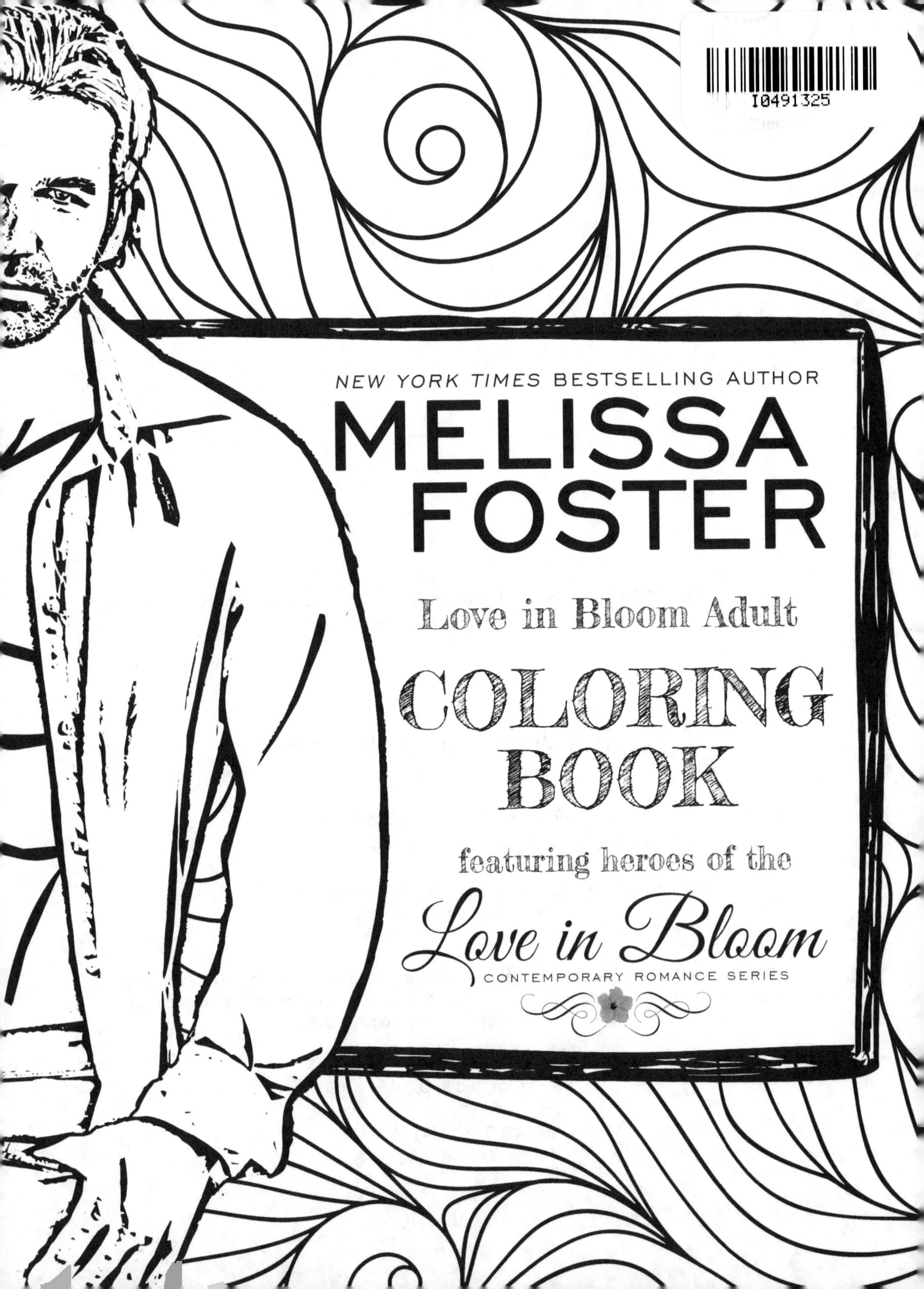

NEW YORK TIMES BESTSELLING AUTHOR

MELISSA FOSTER

Love in Bloom Adult

COLORING BOOK

featuring heroes of the

Love in Bloom

CONTEMPORARY ROMANCE SERIES

DISCLAIMER: This coloring book does NOT contain ALL of the heroes from the Love in Bloom series.

Love in Bloom Adult Coloring Book

Copyright © 2016 by Melissa Foster

www.melissafoster.com

Cover and illustrations by: Jessica Hildreth at Creative Book Concepts

jessicahildrethdesigns.com

Printed in U.S.A

ISBN-13:978-1-941480-64-9
ISBN-10:1-941480-64-0

Dear Colorists,

I hope you enjoy your Love in Bloom coloring book and creating your own versions of our hunky heroes. Please note that all of the hunky heroes of the Love in Bloom family are not depicted in these pages because the series is continually growing.

For more information about Love in Bloom and the rest of my steamy romance novels, please visit my website. www.MelissaFoster.com

Happy coloring,

Melissa Foster

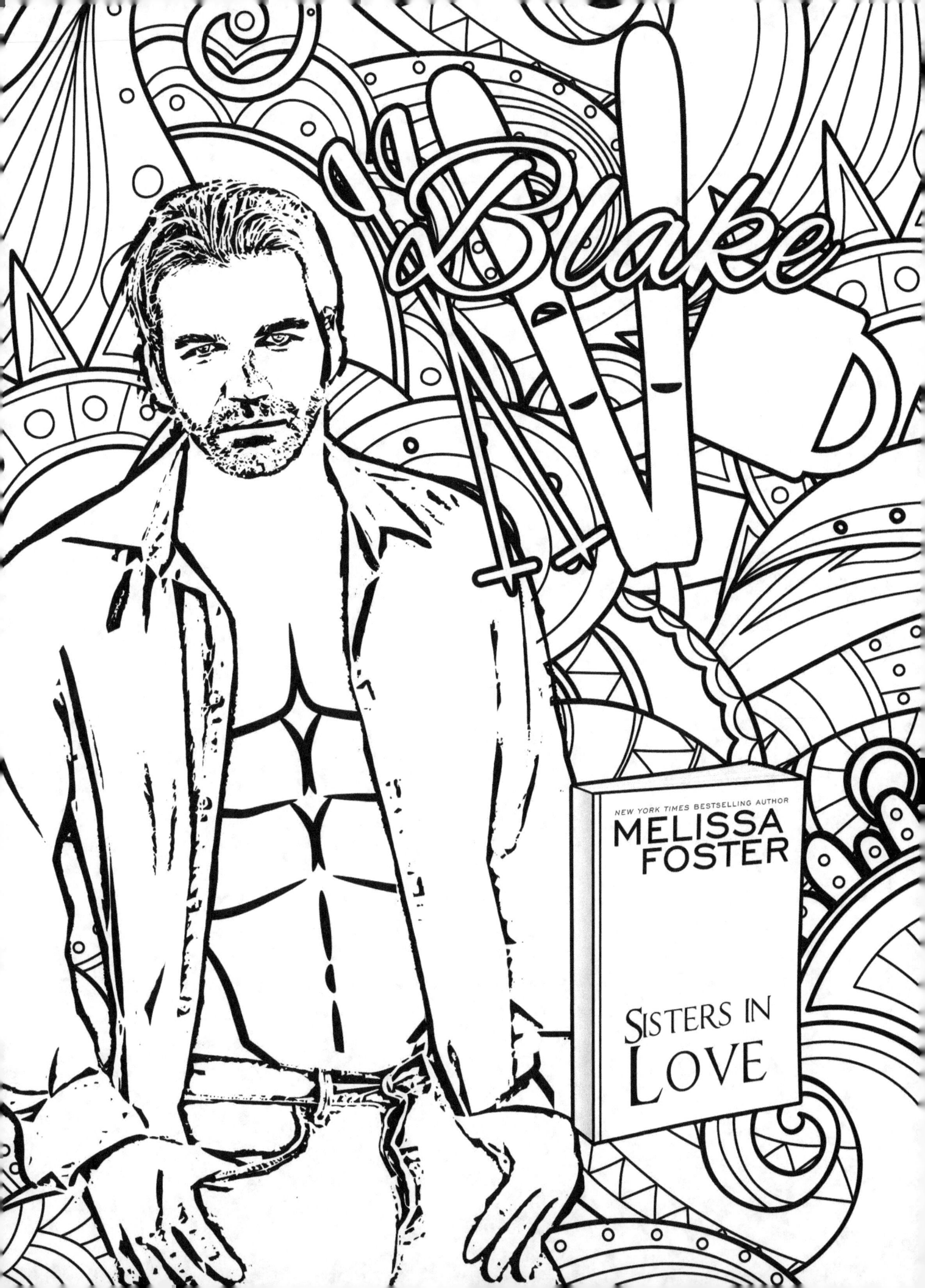

Blake

NEW YORK TIMES BESTSELLING AUTHOR
MELISSA FOSTER

SISTERS IN LOVE

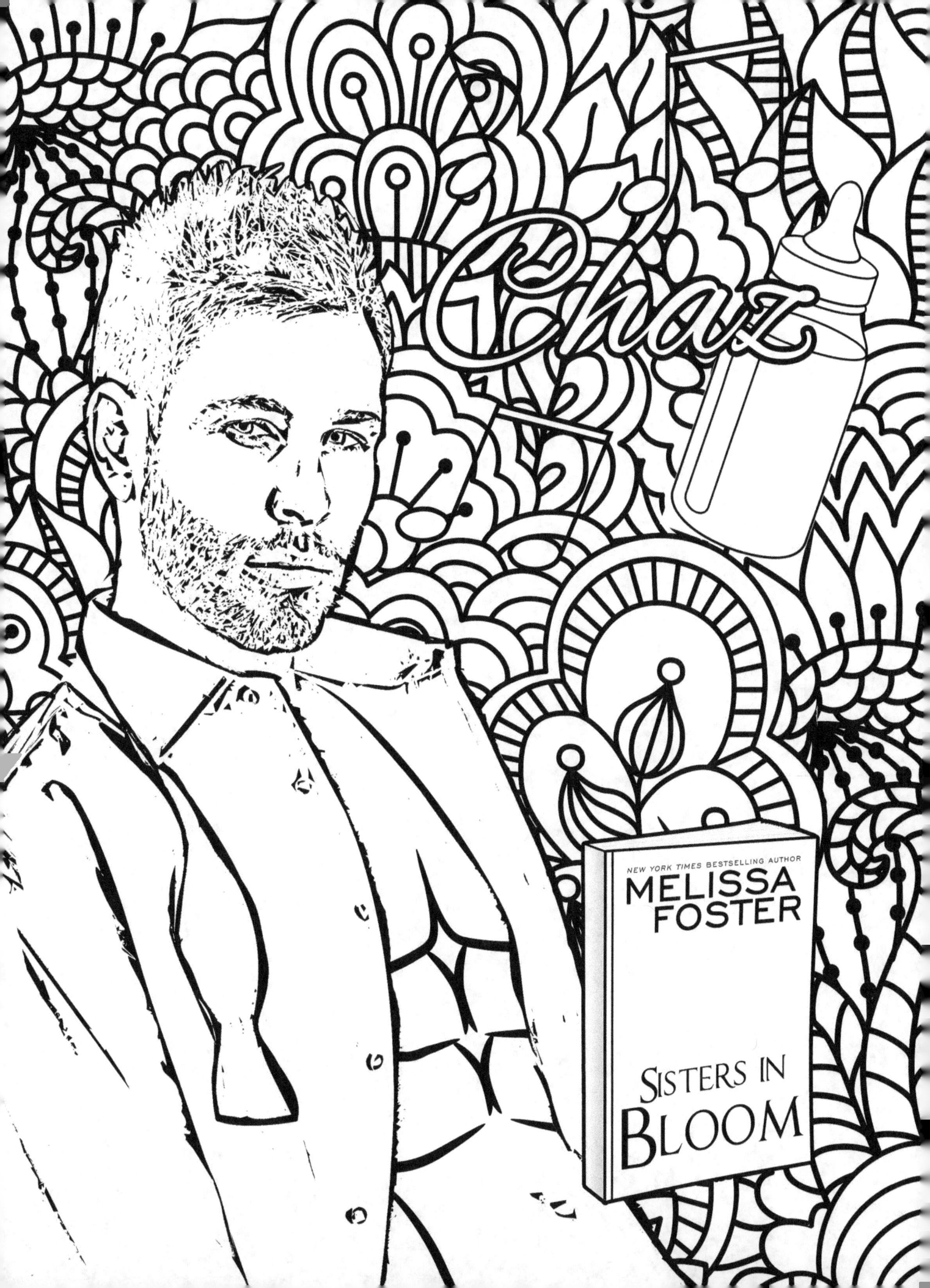

Chaz

NEW YORK TIMES BESTSELLING AUTHOR
MELISSA
FOSTER

SISTERS IN
BLOOM

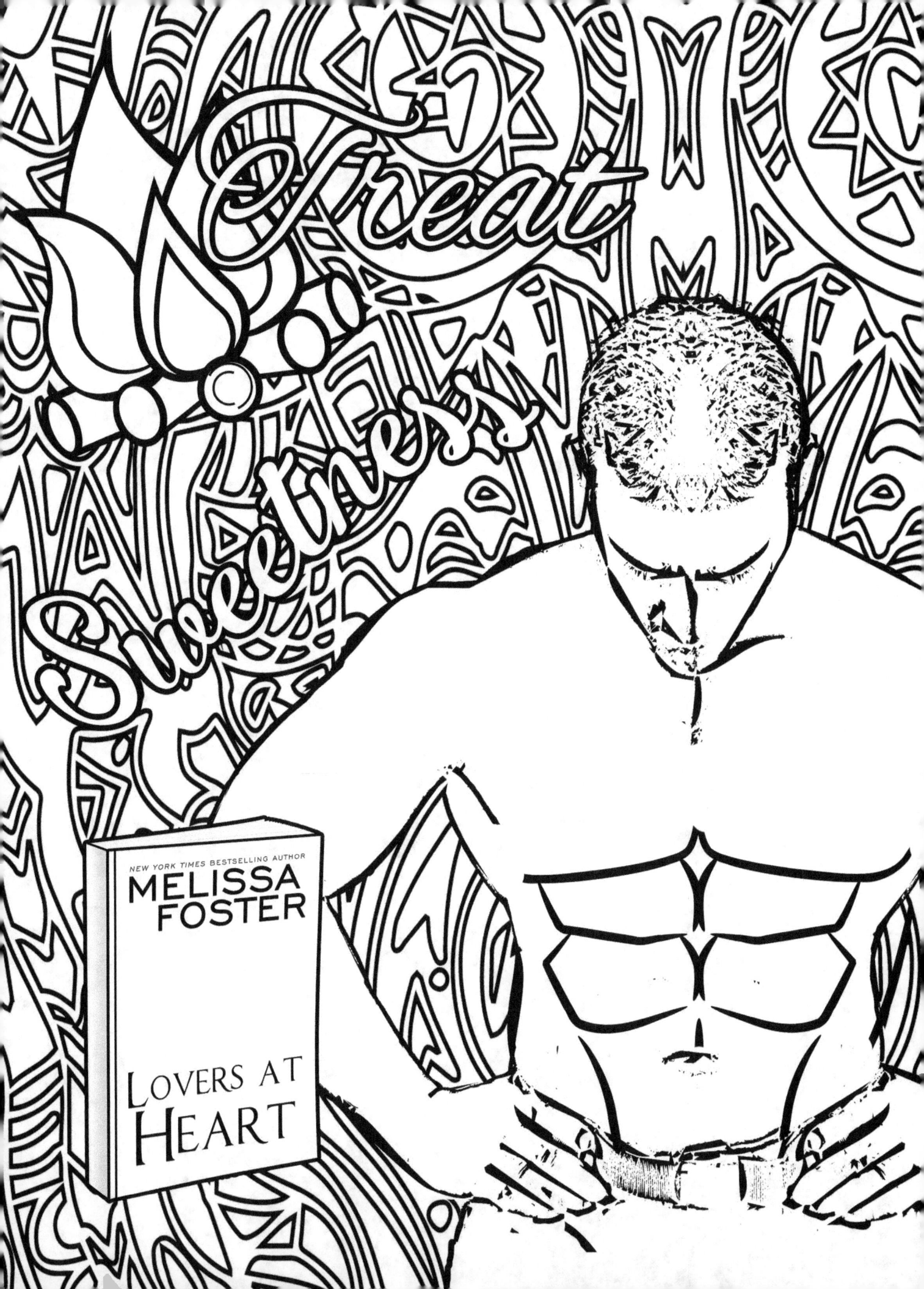

Treat

Sweetness

NEW YORK TIMES BESTSELLING AUTHOR
MELISSA FOSTER

LOVERS AT
HEART

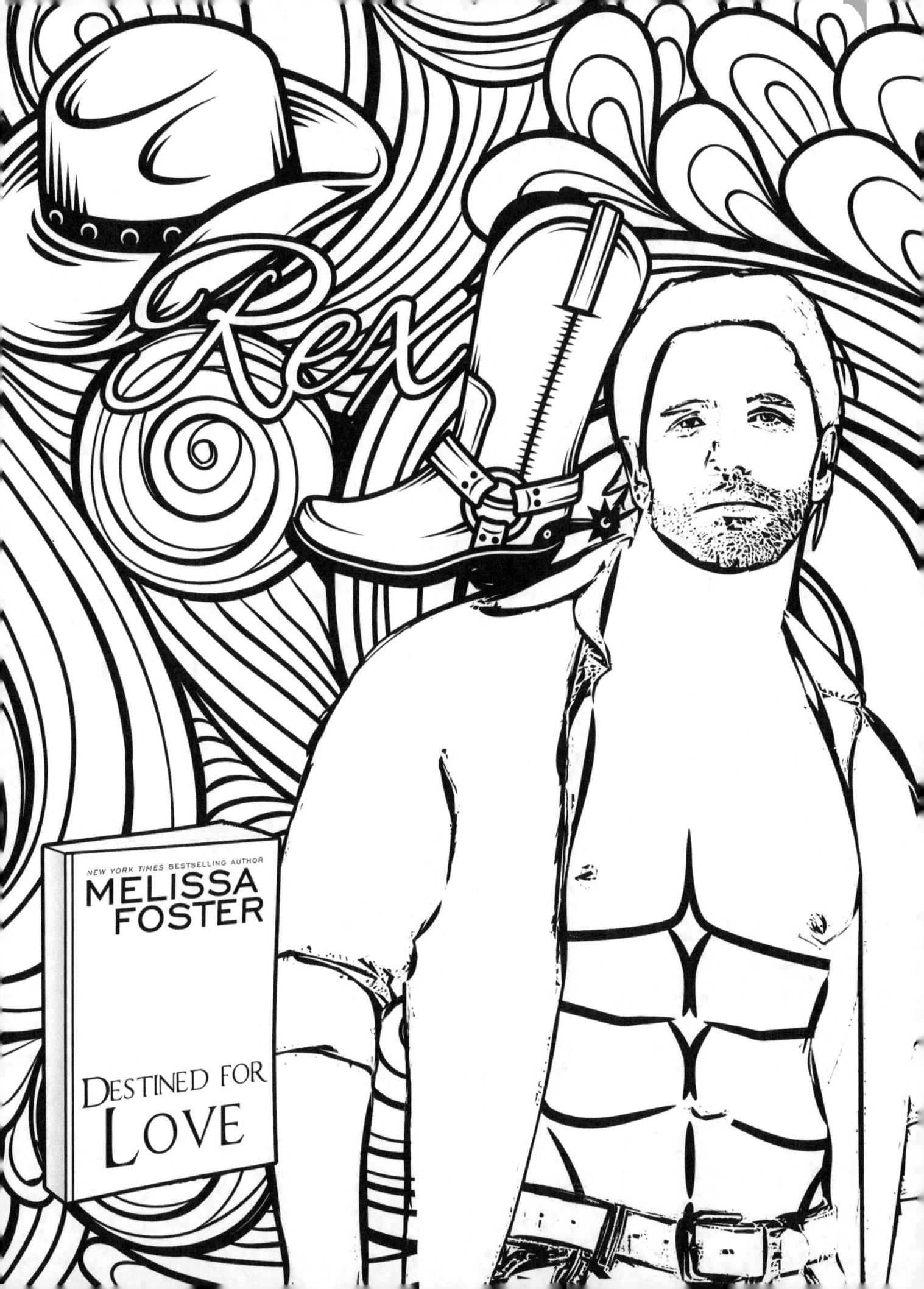

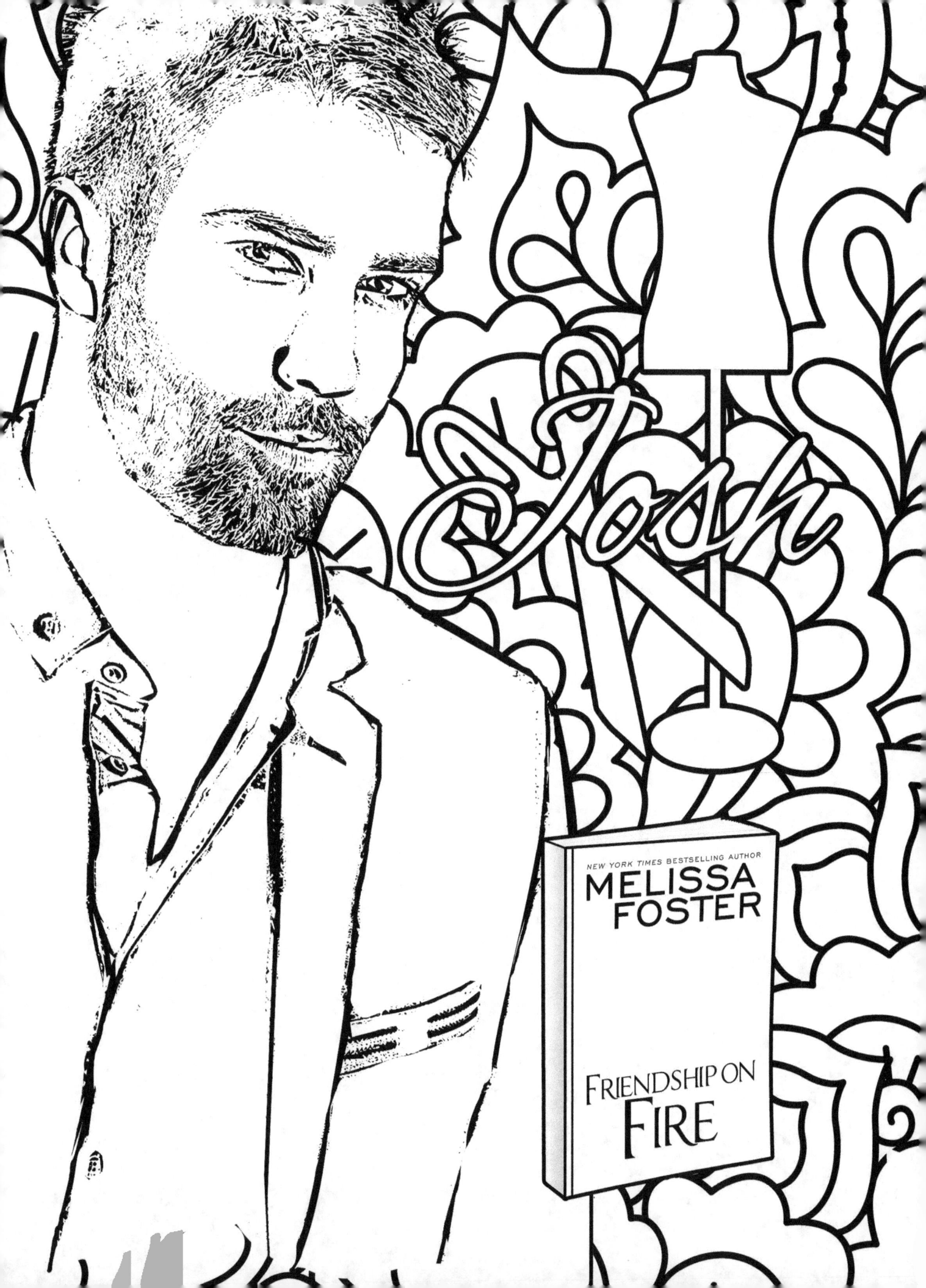

Josh

NEW YORK TIMES BESTSELLING AUTHOR
MELISSA FOSTER

FRIENDSHIP ON
FIRE

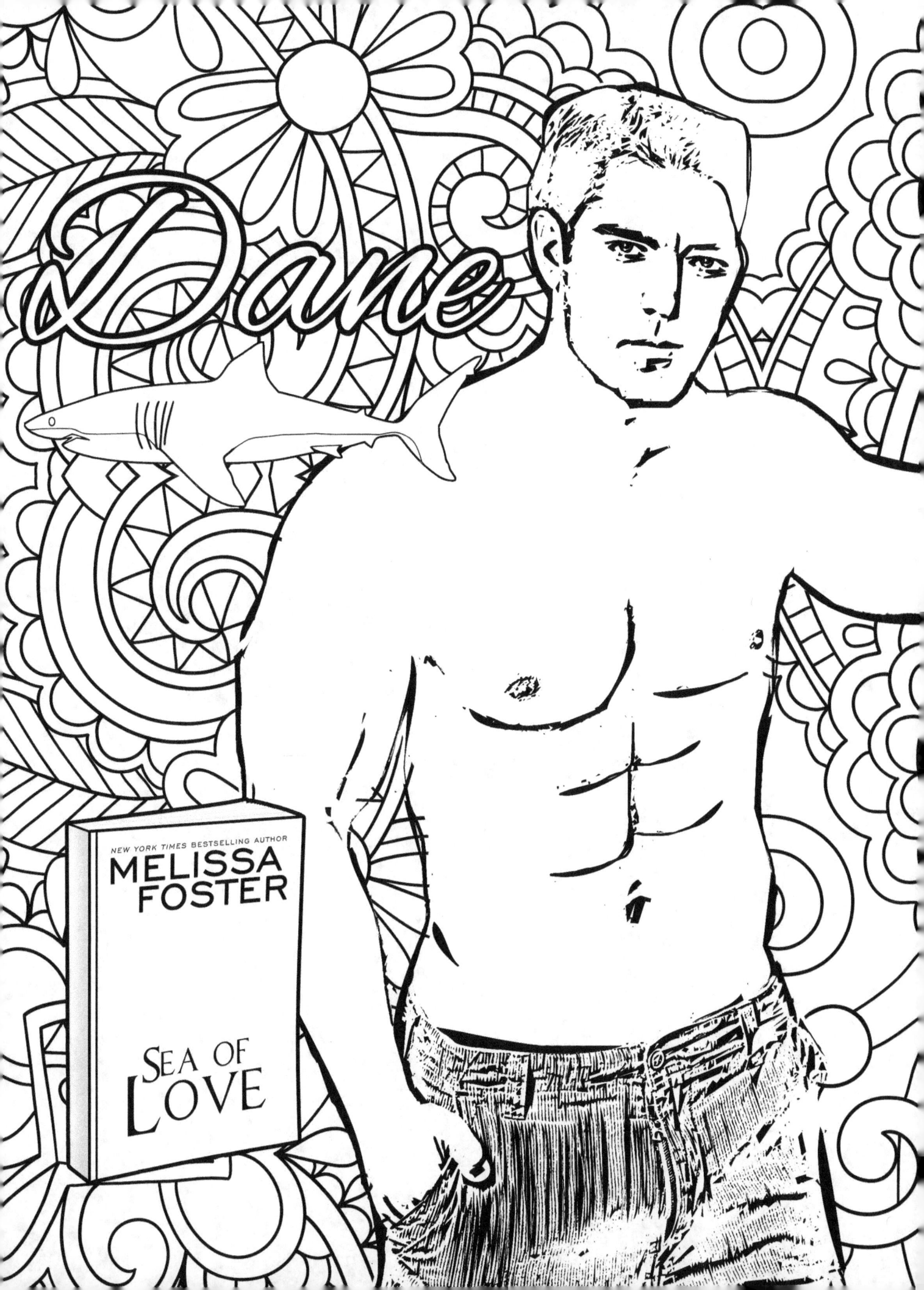

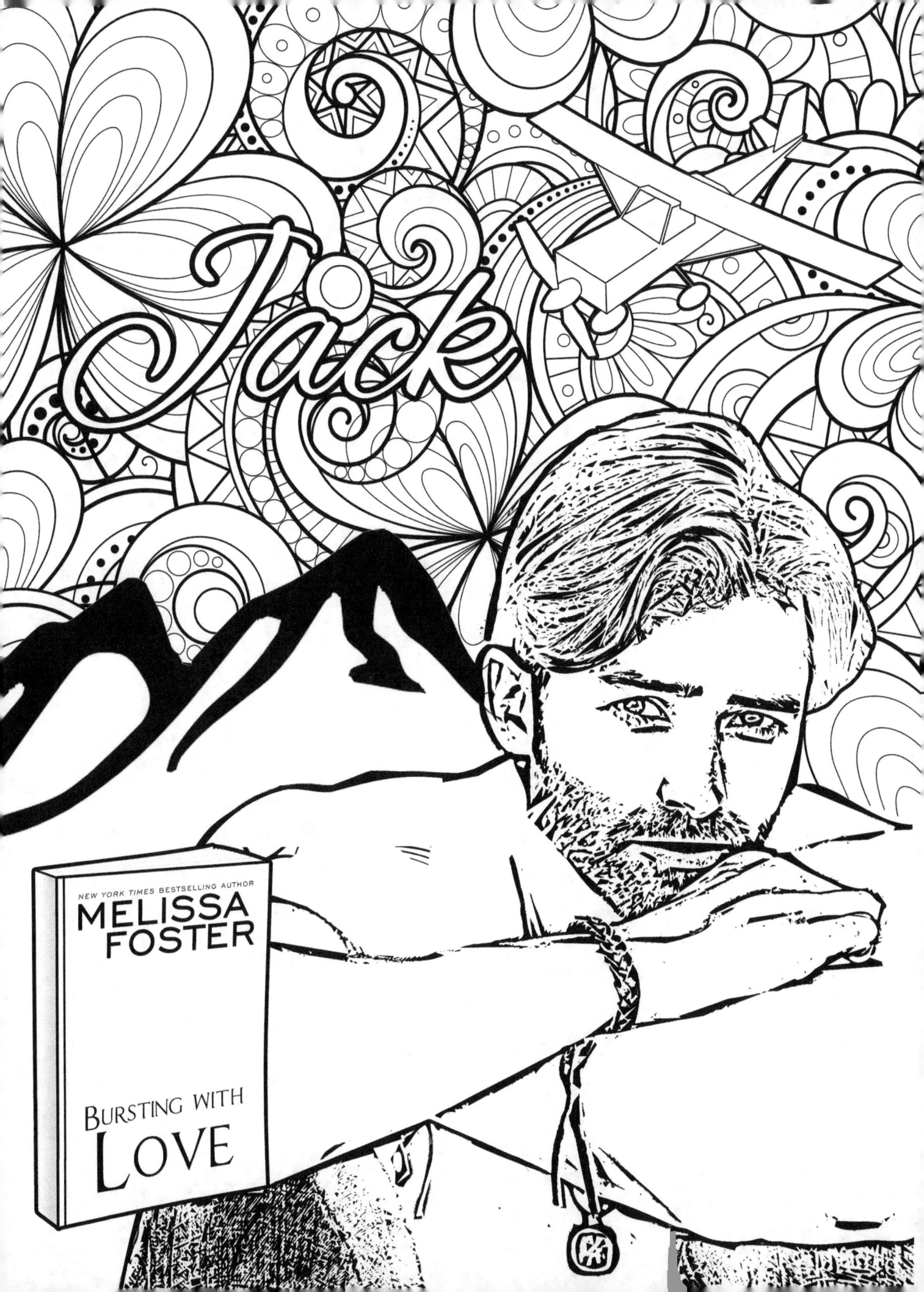

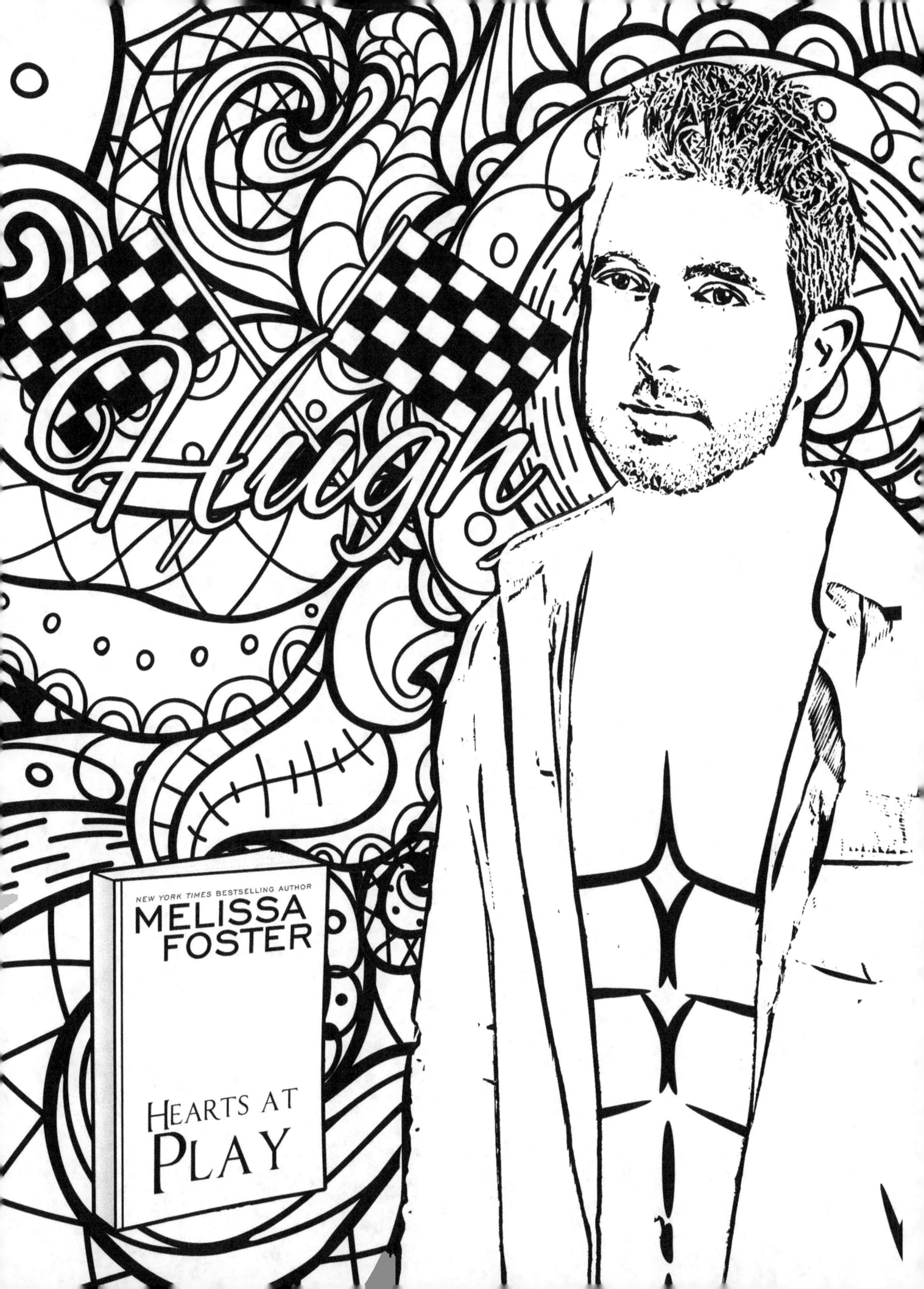

Hugh

NEW YORK TIMES BESTSELLING AUTHOR

MELISSA
FOSTER

HEARTS AT
PLAY

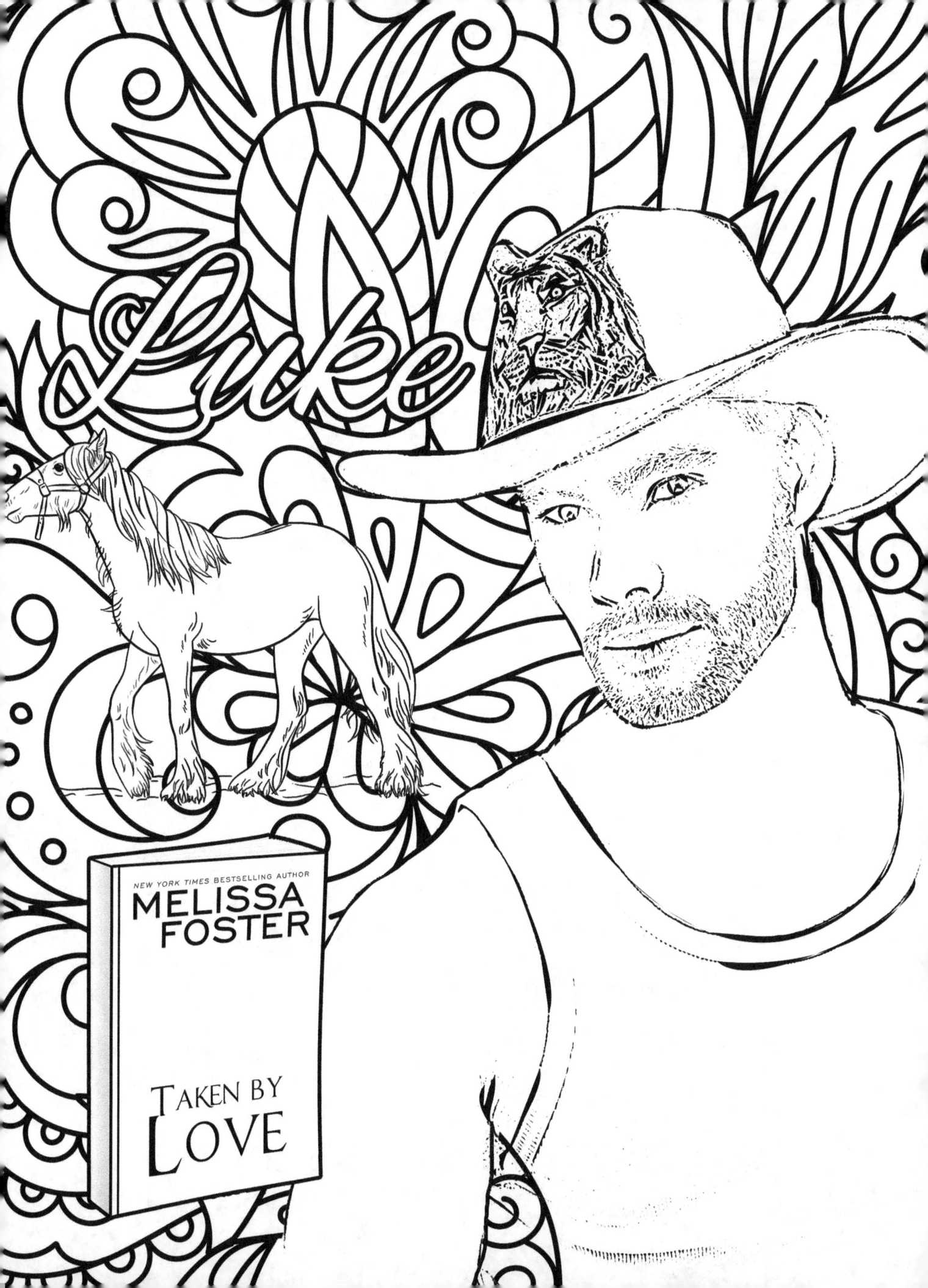

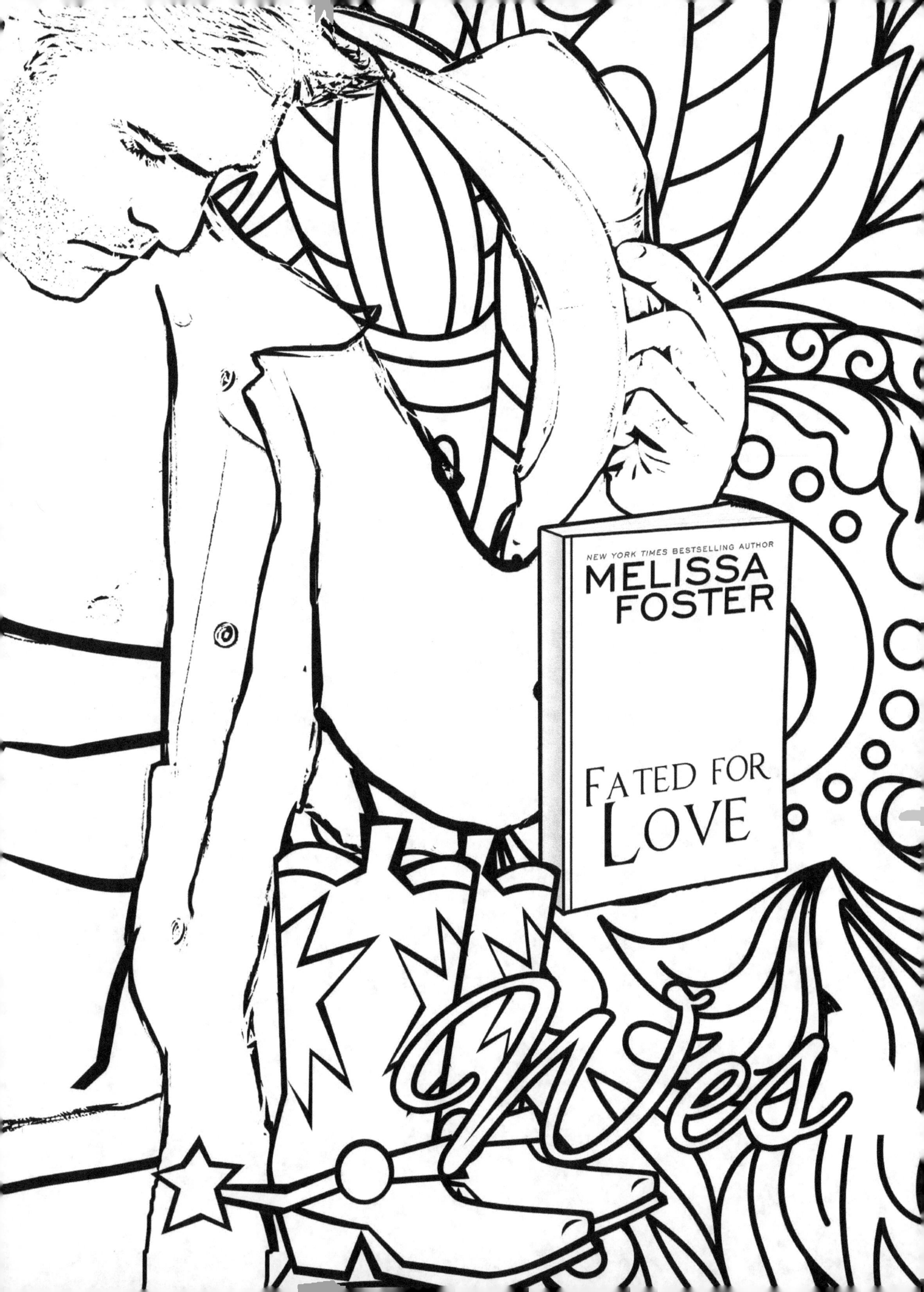

NEW YORK TIMES BESTSELLING AUTHOR

MELISSA FOSTER

FATED FOR LOVE

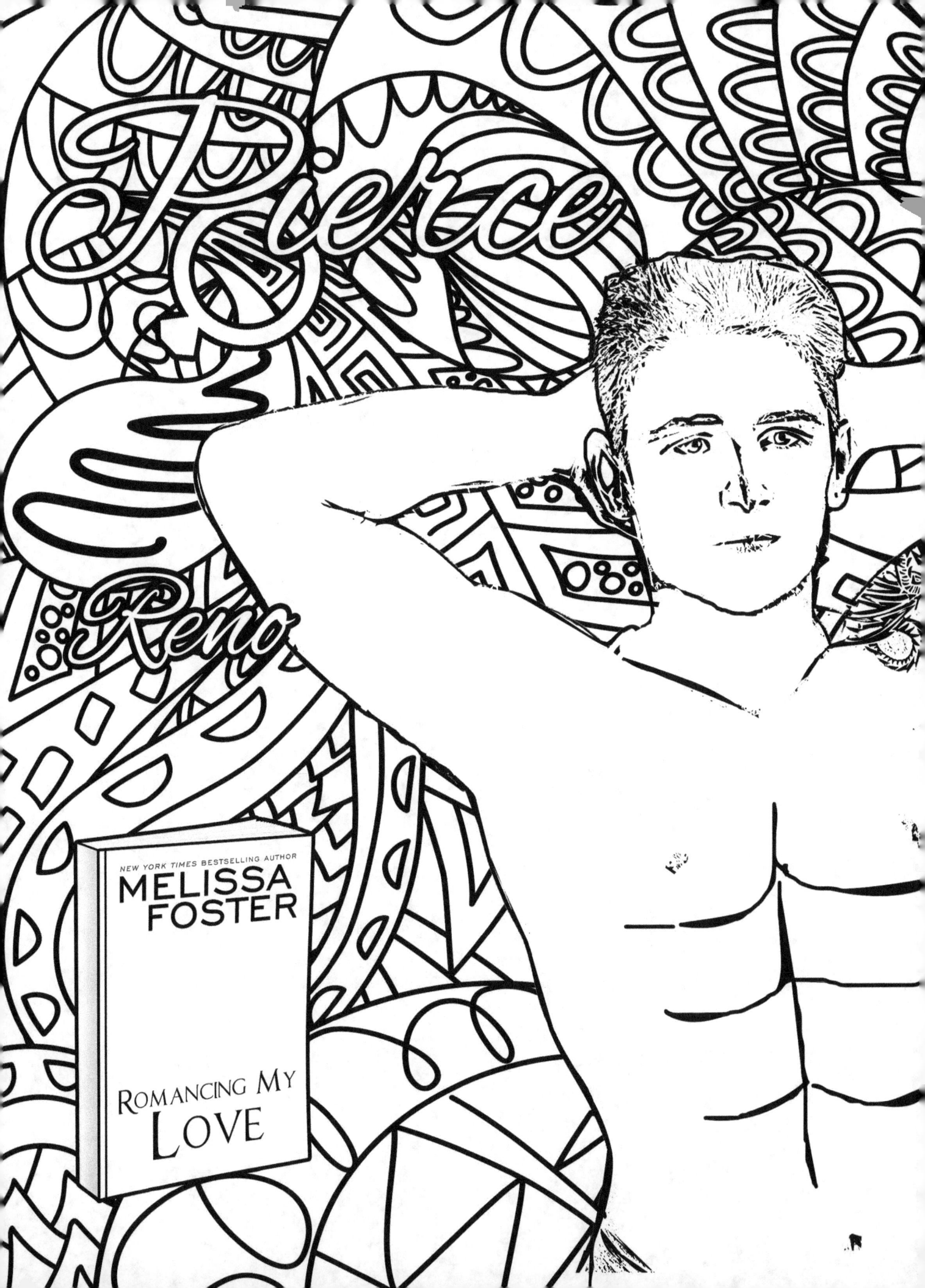

Pierce

Reno

NEW YORK TIMES BESTSELLING AUTHOR

MELISSA
FOSTER

ROMANCING MY
LOVE

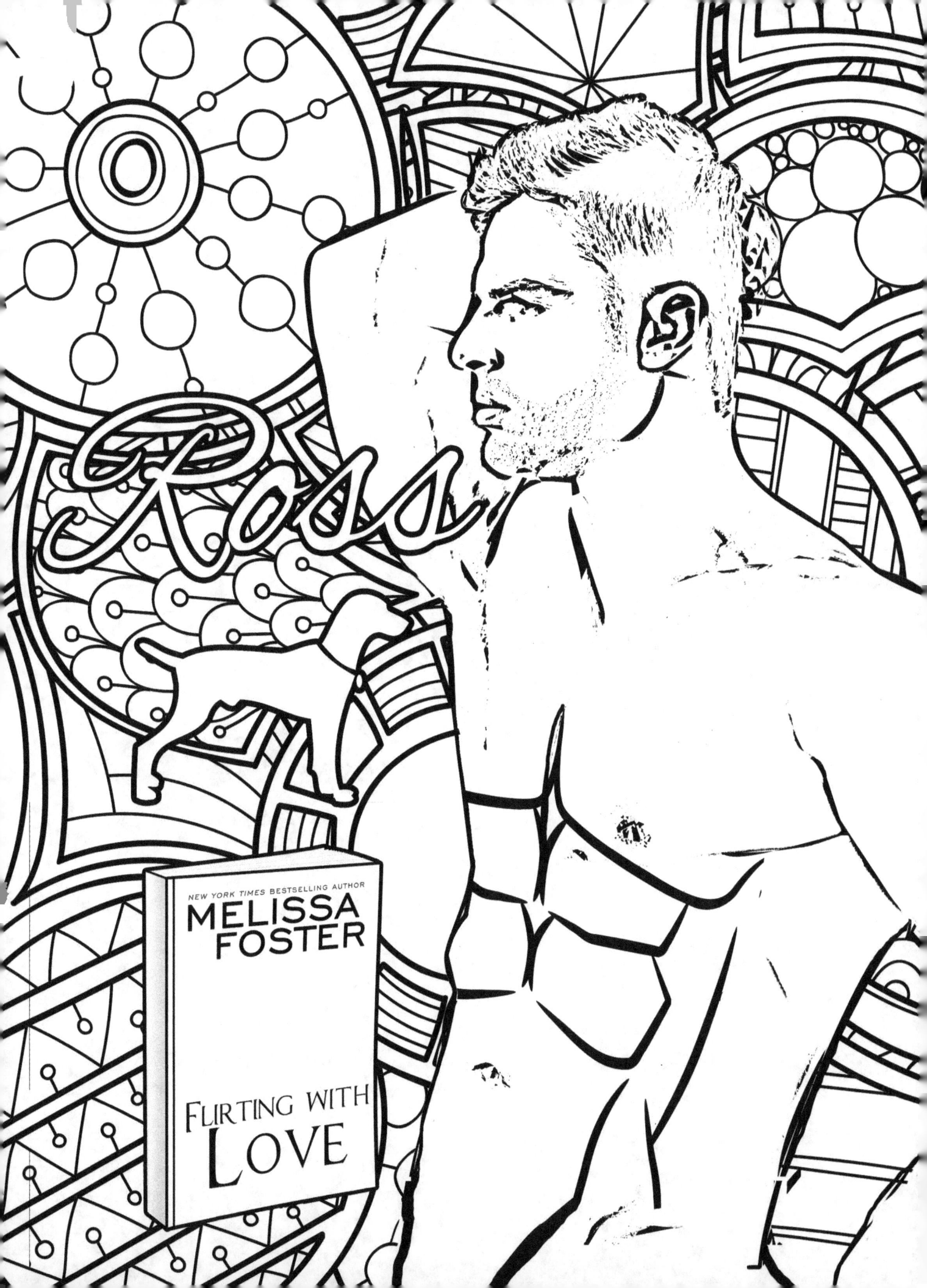

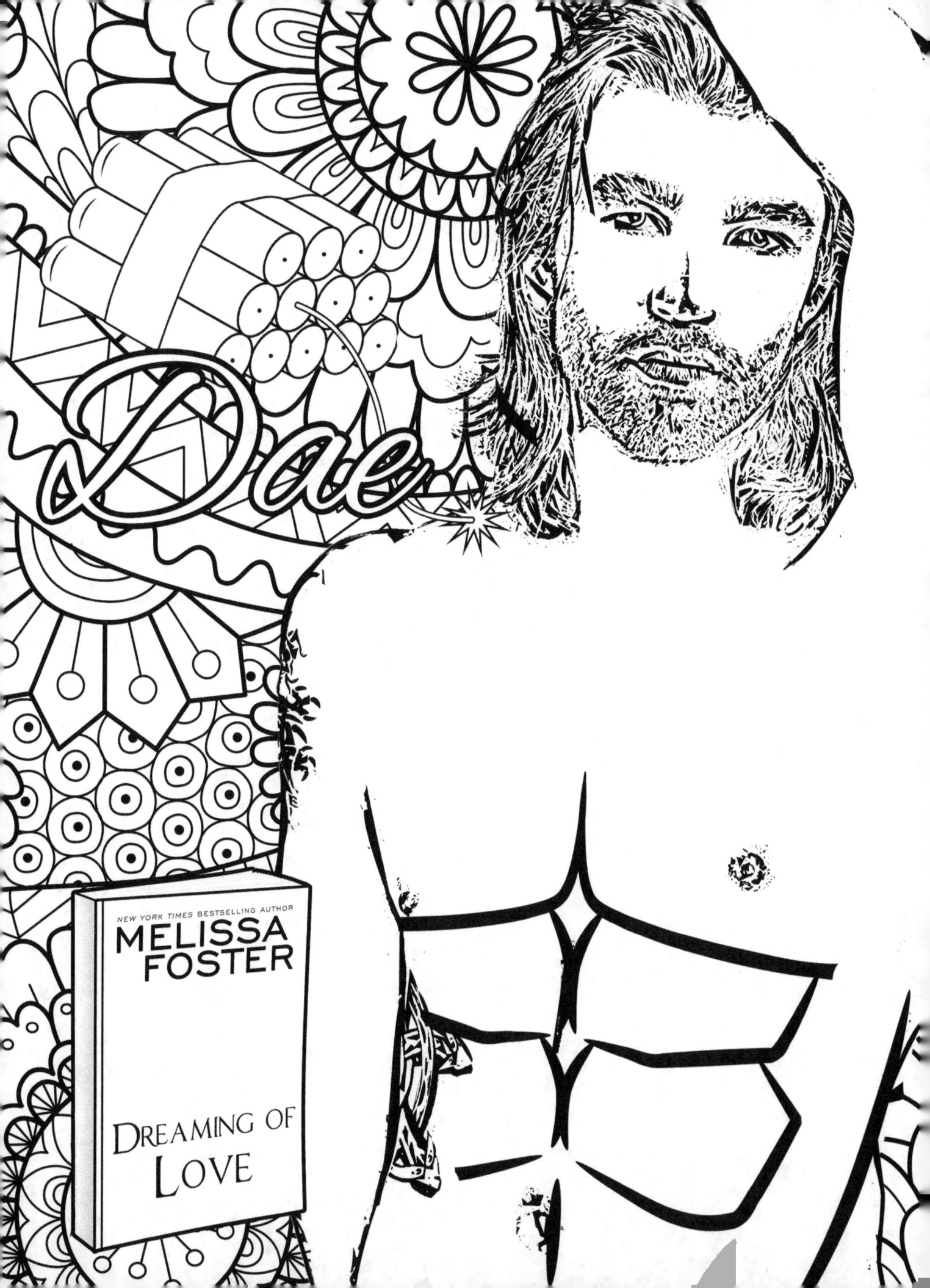

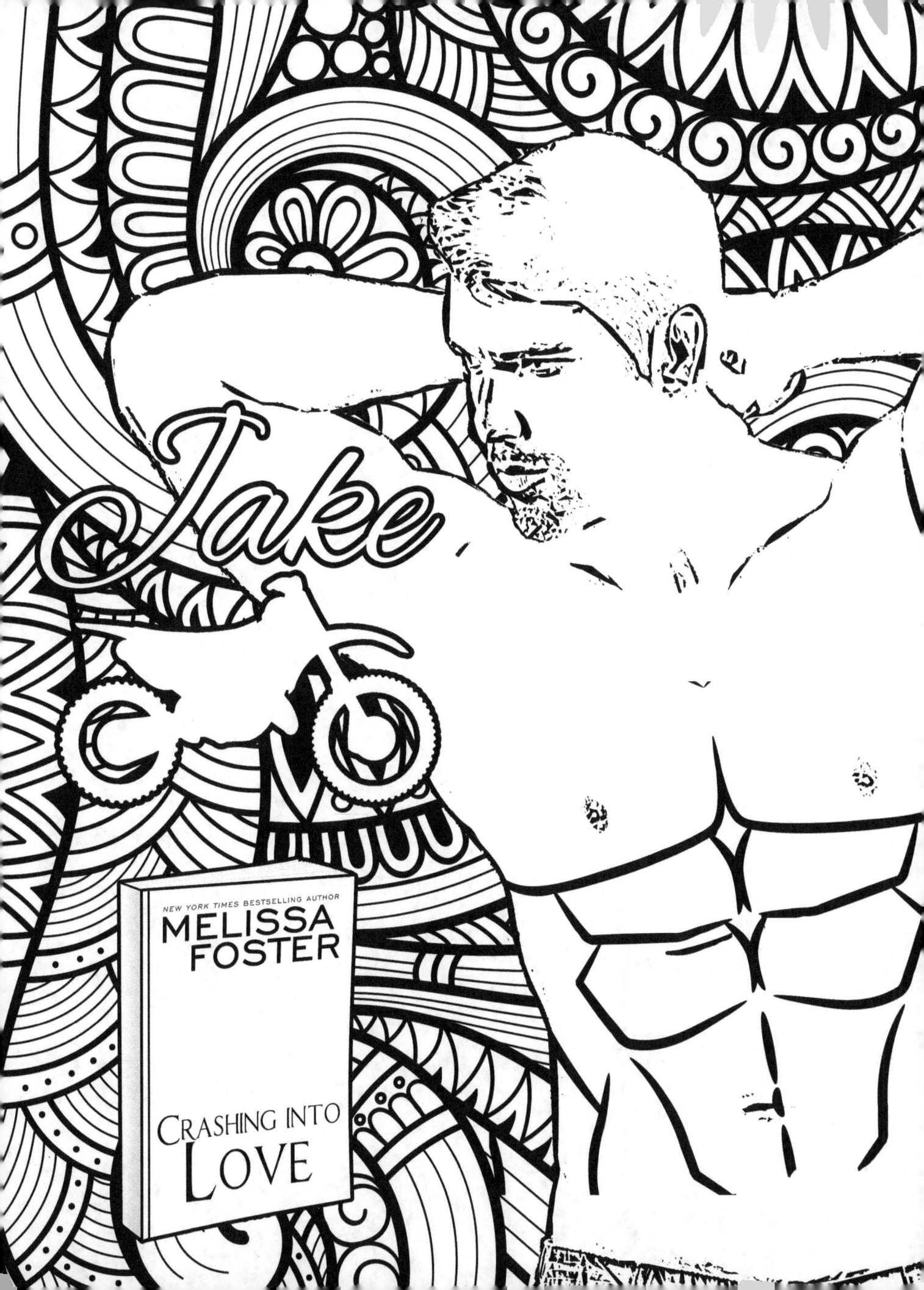

Jake

NEW YORK TIMES BESTSELLING AUTHOR
MELISSA
FOSTER

CRASHING INTO
LOVE

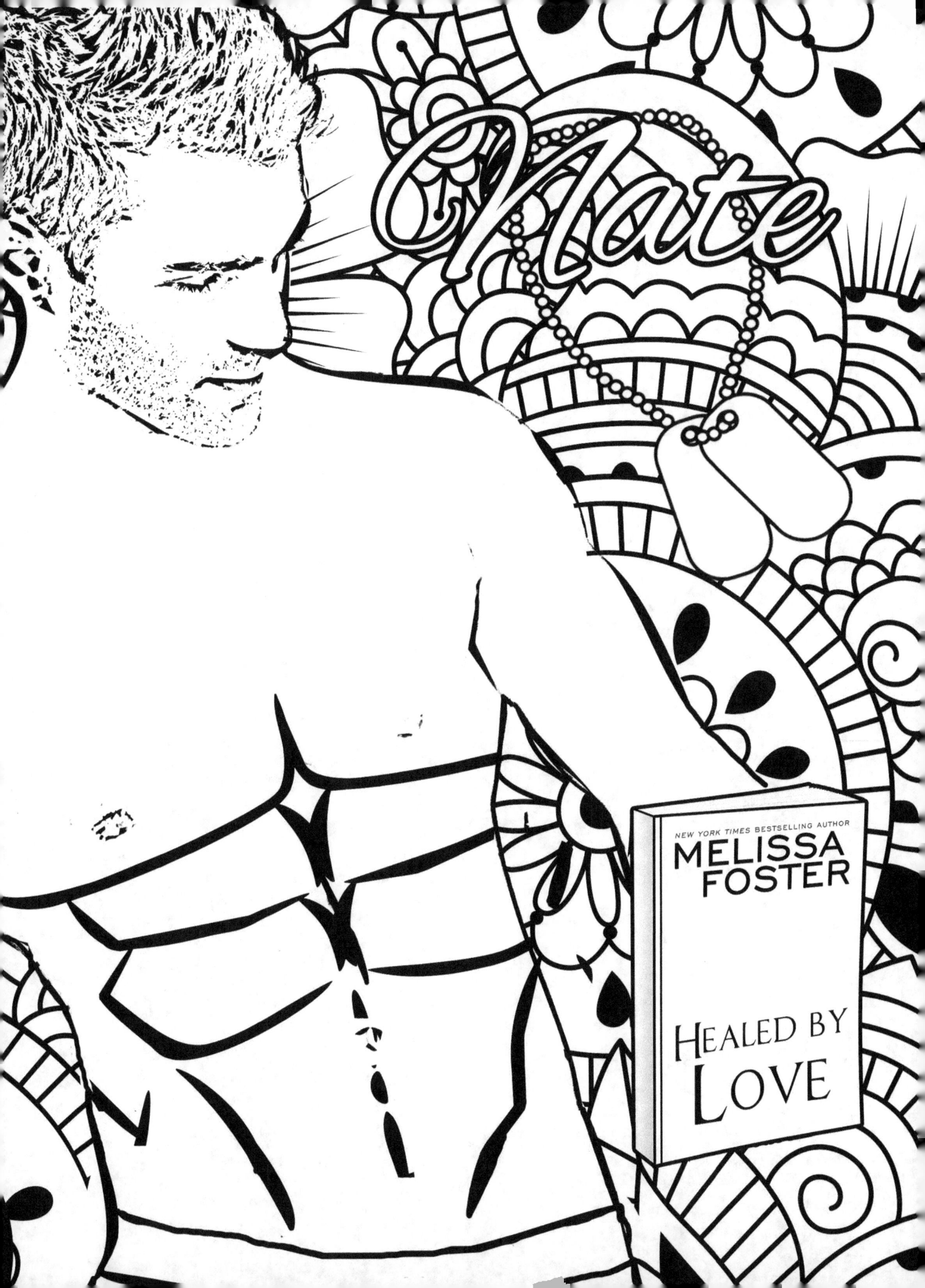

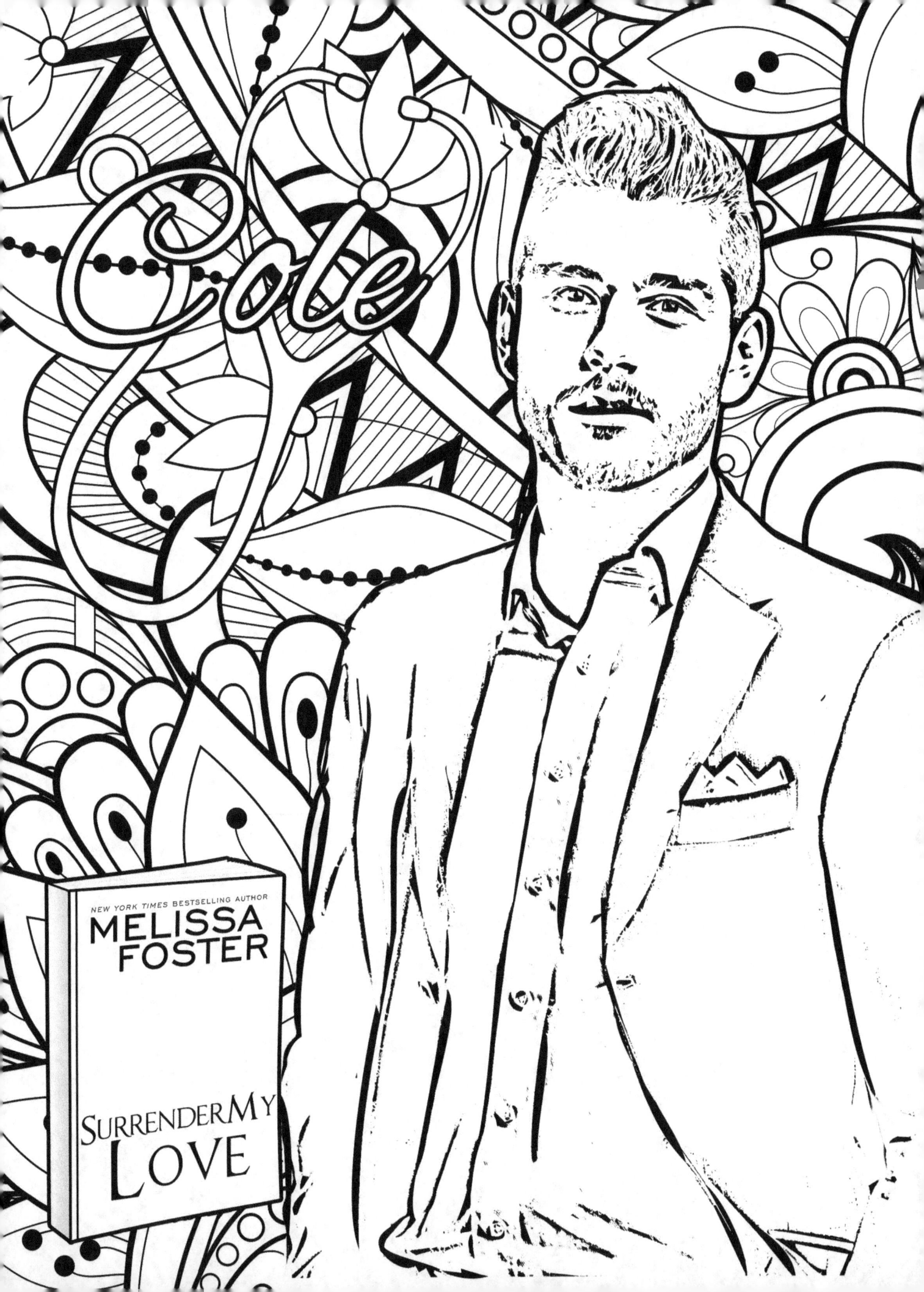

Cole

NEW YORK TIMES BESTSELLING AUTHOR
MELISSA
FOSTER

SURRENDER MY
LOVE

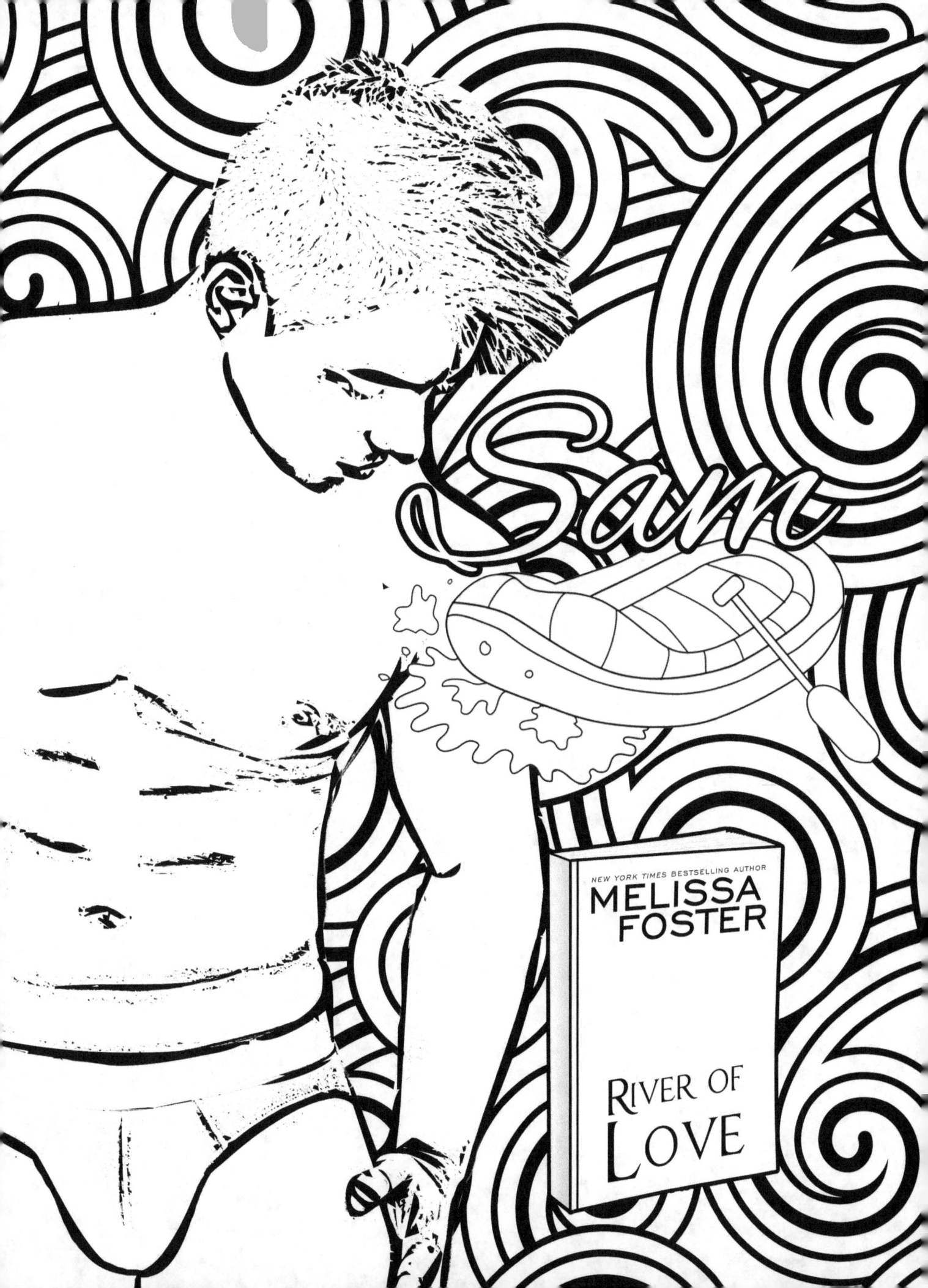

Sam

NEW YORK TIMES BESTSELLING AUTHOR
MELISSA FOSTER

RIVER OF LOVE

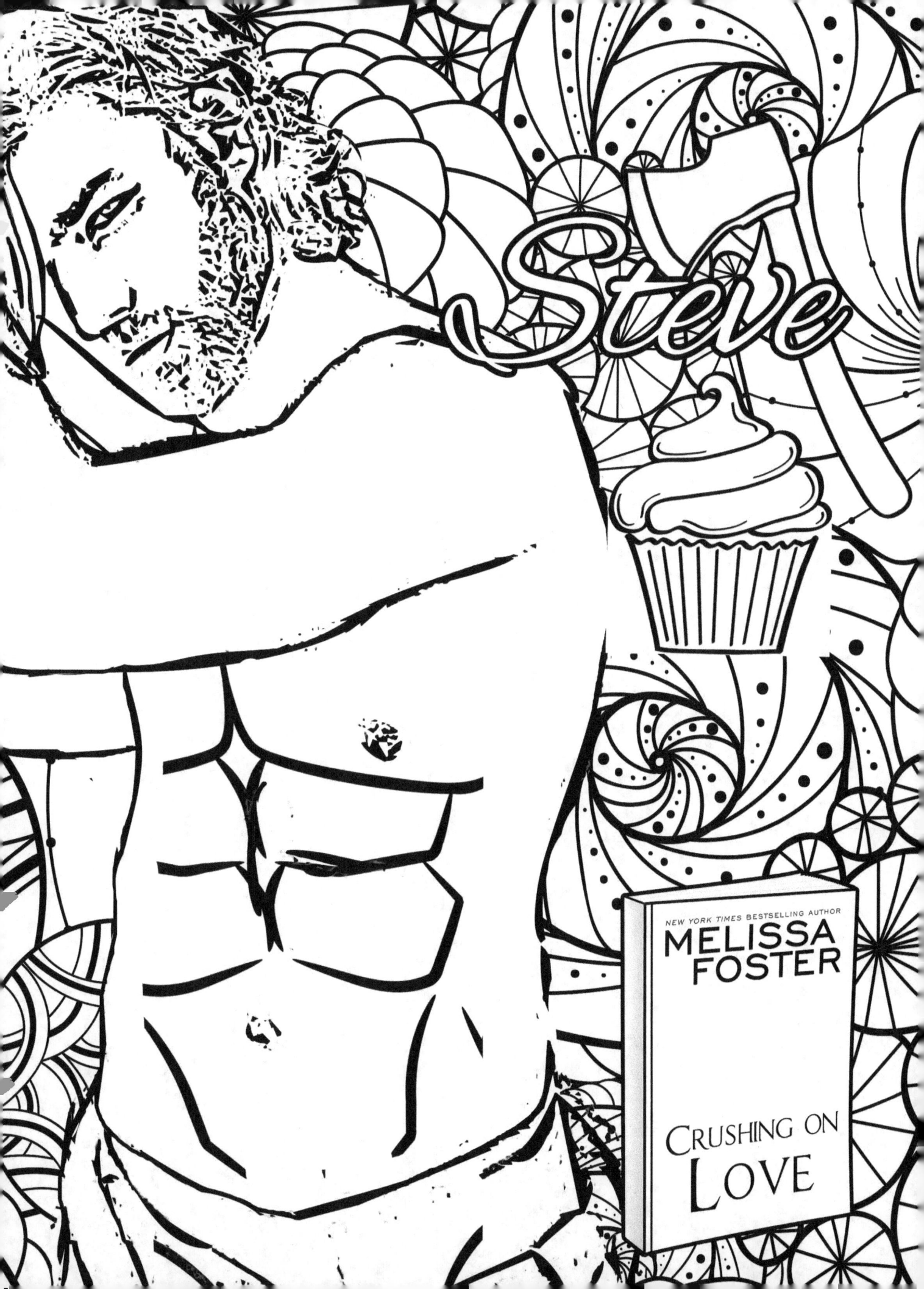

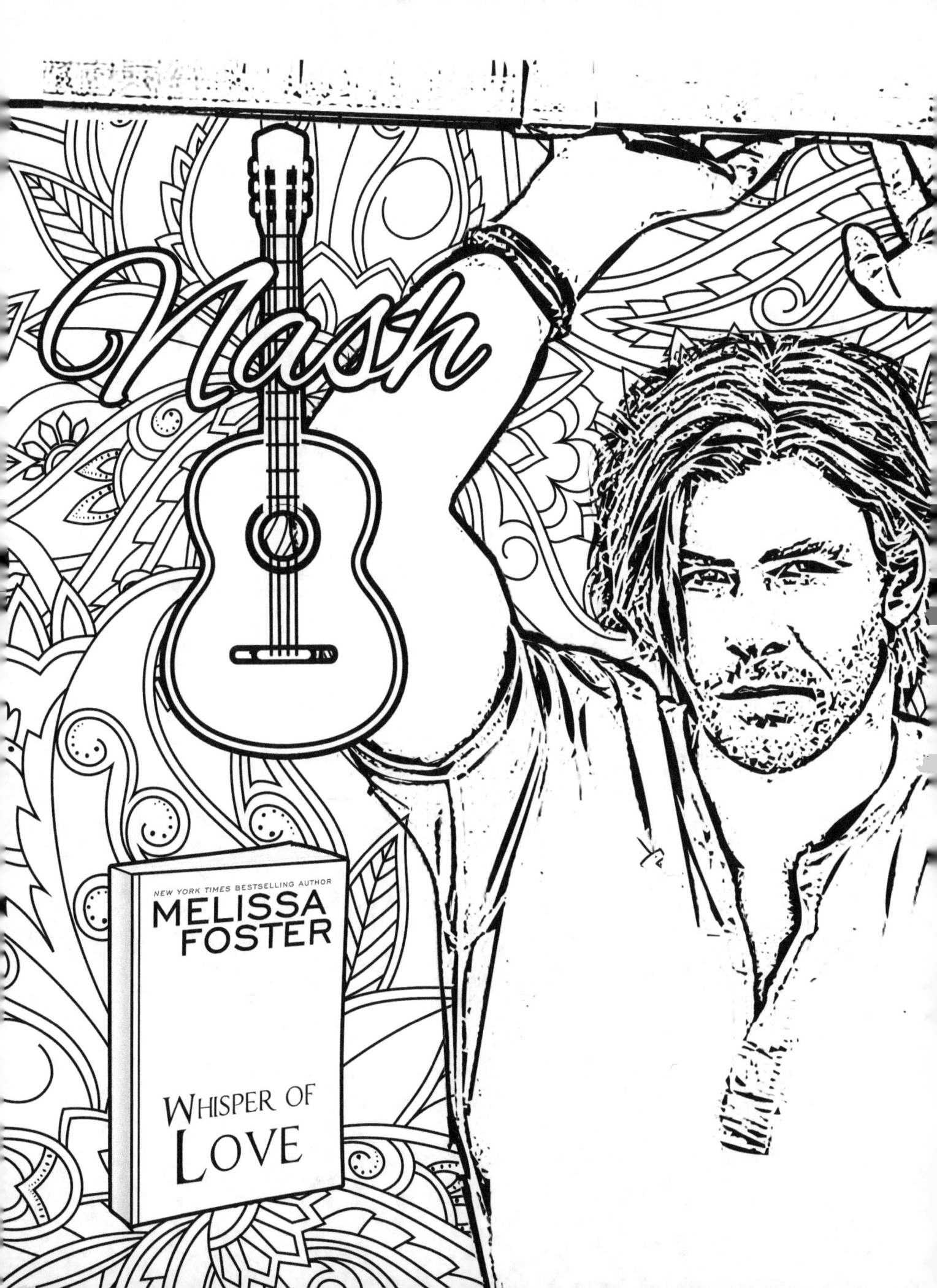

Nash

NEW YORK TIMES BESTSELLING AUTHOR
MELISSA FOSTER

WHISPER OF
LOVE

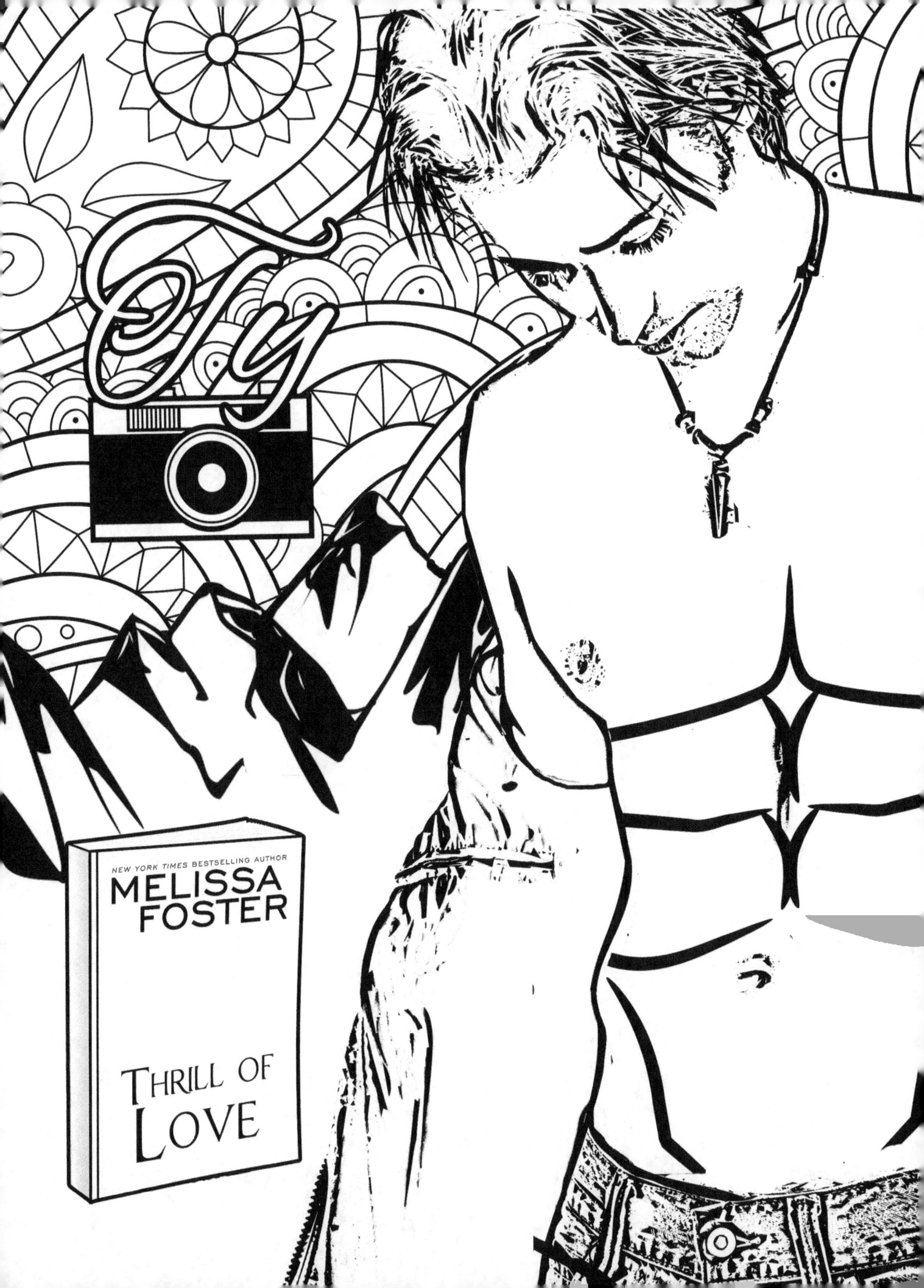

Ty

NEW YORK TIMES BESTSELLING AUTHOR
MELISSA
FOSTER

THRILL OF
LOVE

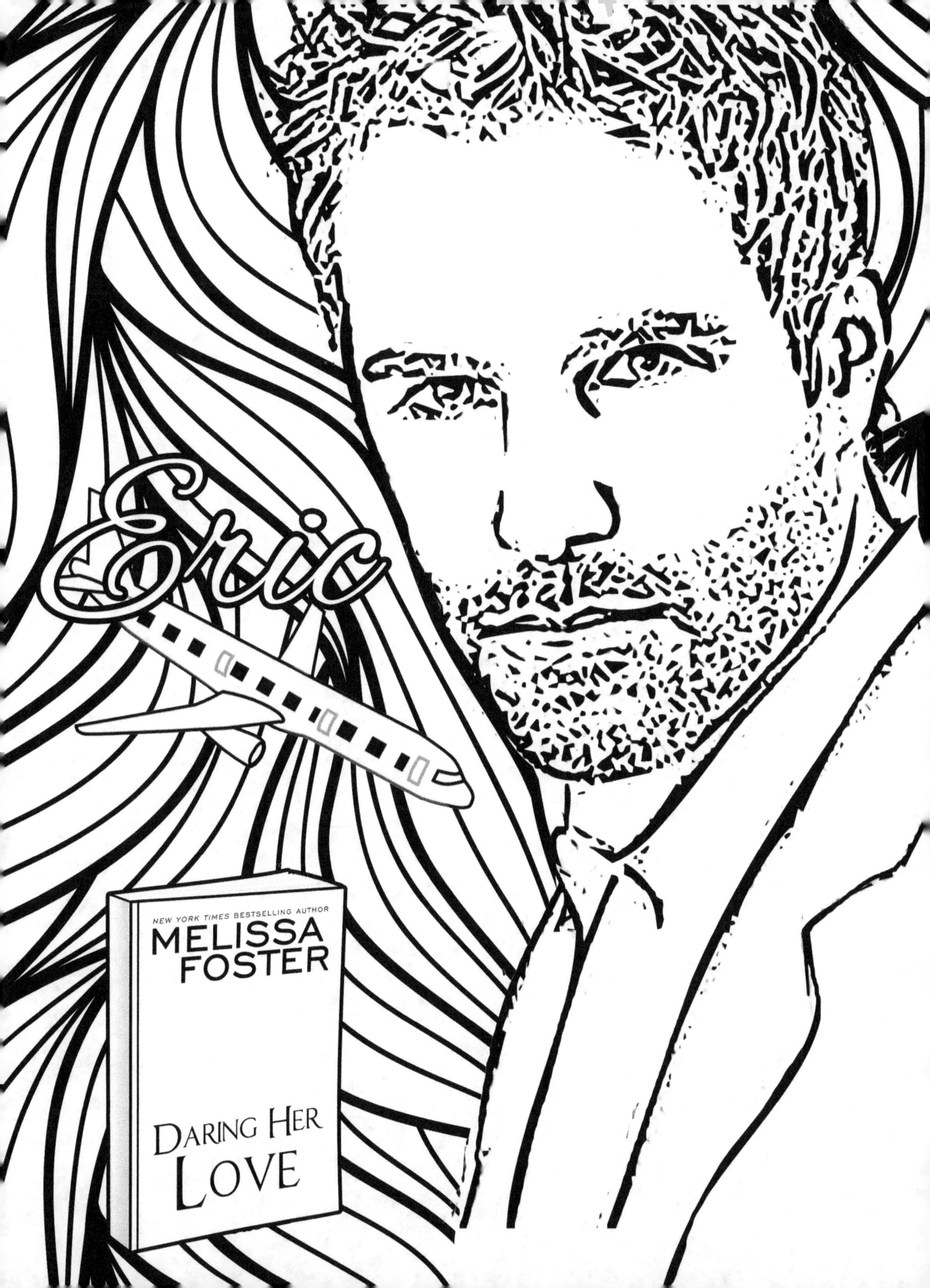

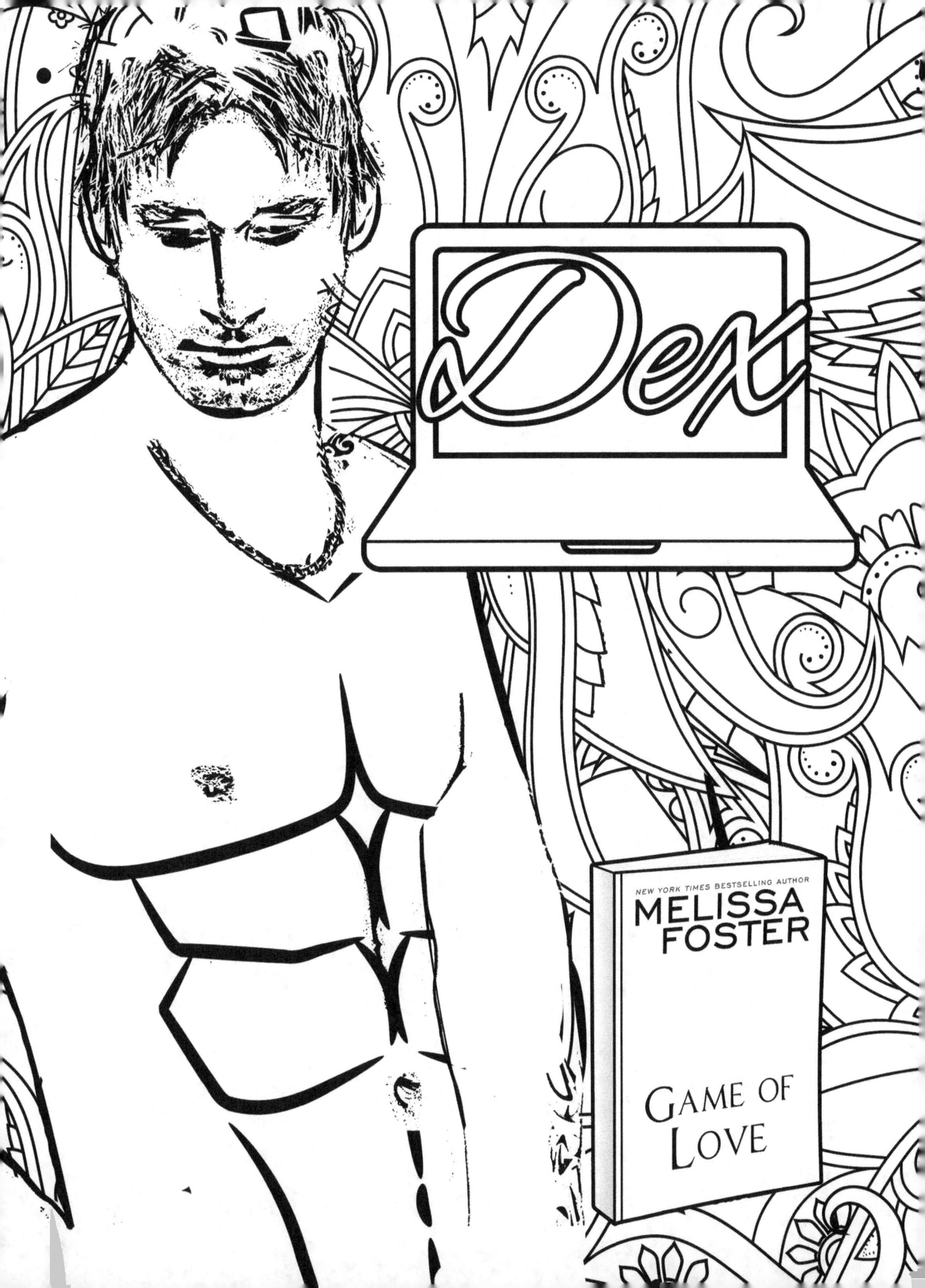

Dex

NEW YORK TIMES BESTSELLING AUTHOR
MELISSA FOSTER

GAME OF
LOVE

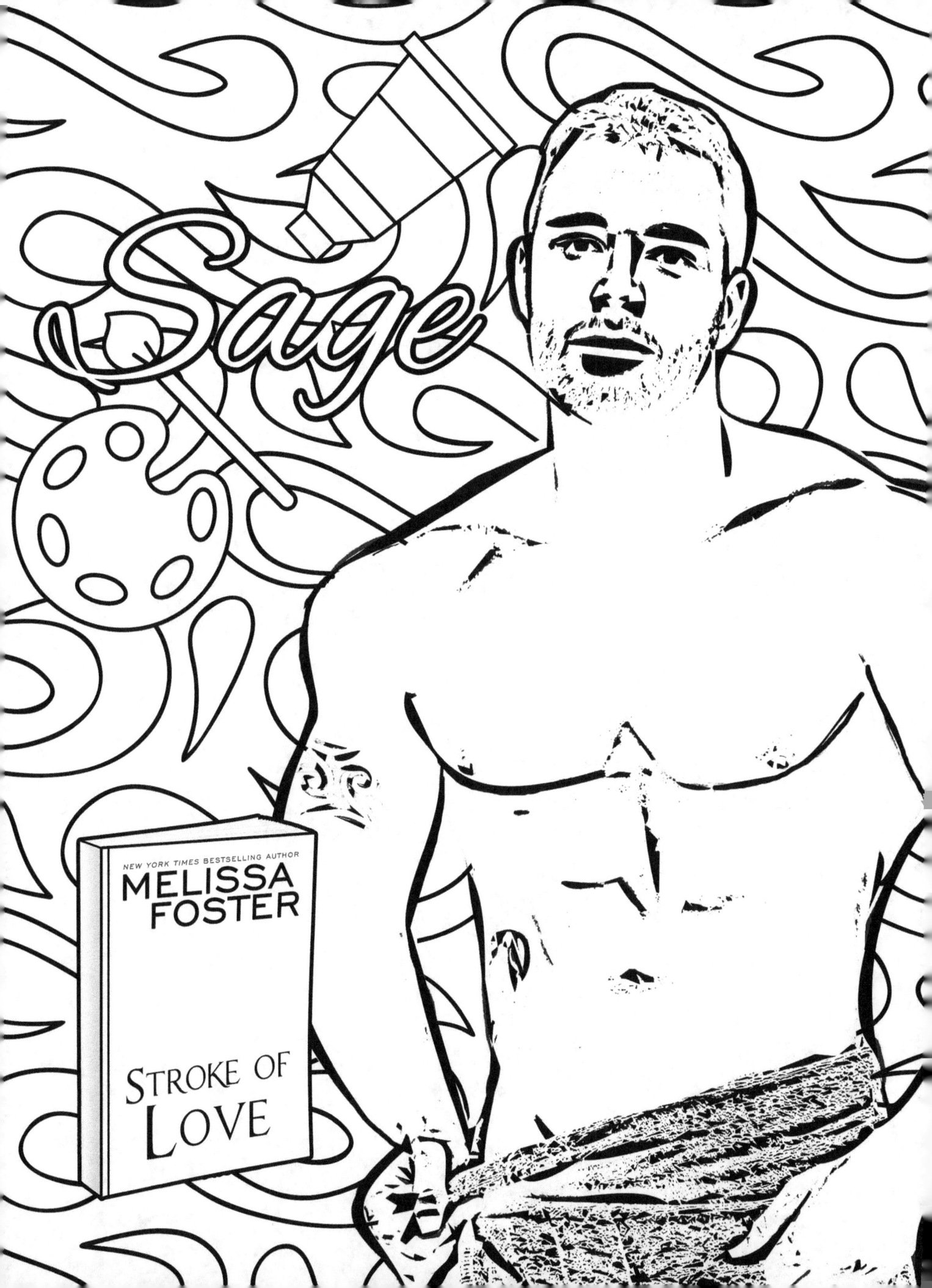

Sage

NEW YORK TIMES BESTSELLING AUTHOR
MELISSA
FOSTER

STROKE OF
LOVE

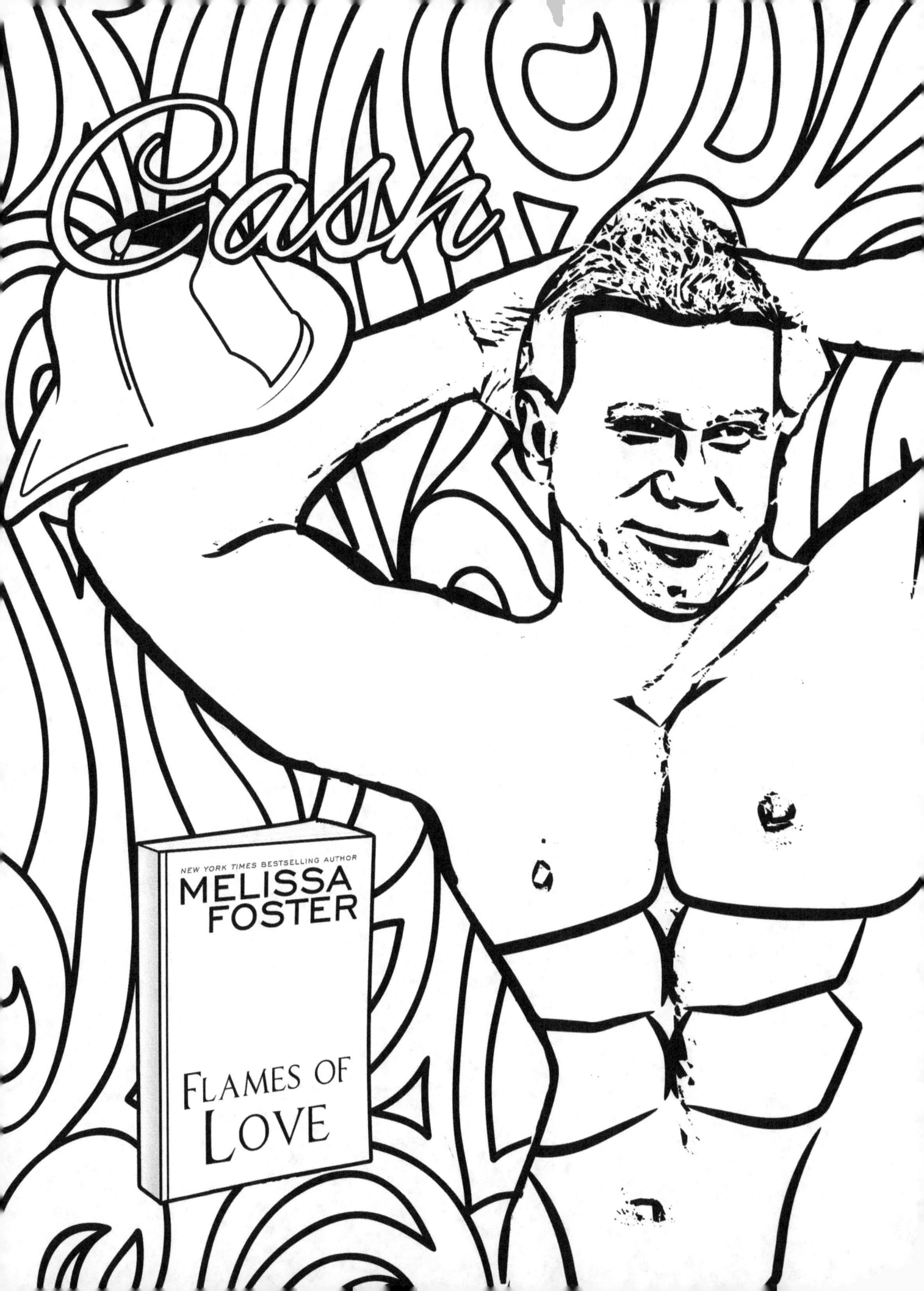

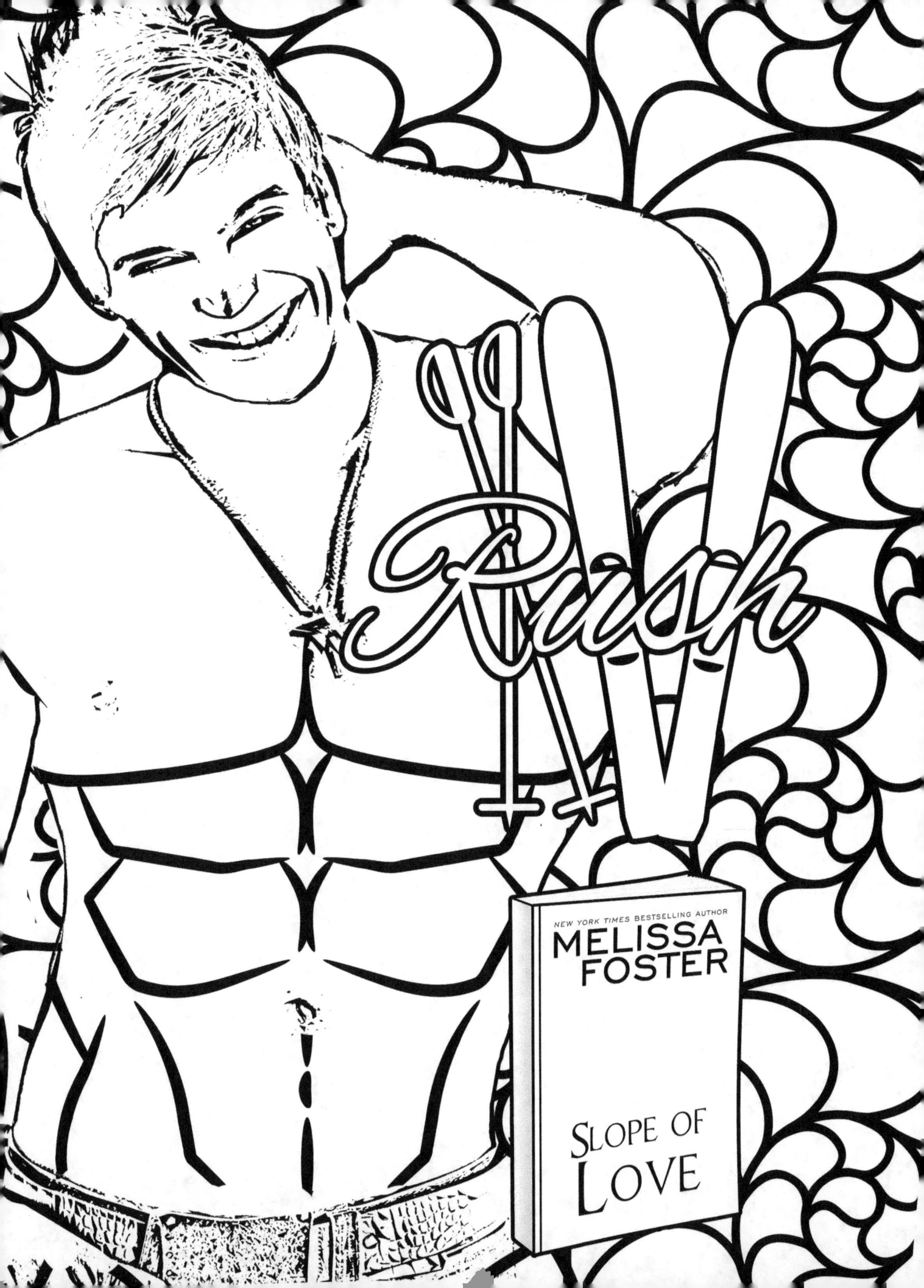

Rush

NEW YORK TIMES BESTSELLING AUTHOR
MELISSA FOSTER

SLOPE OF LOVE

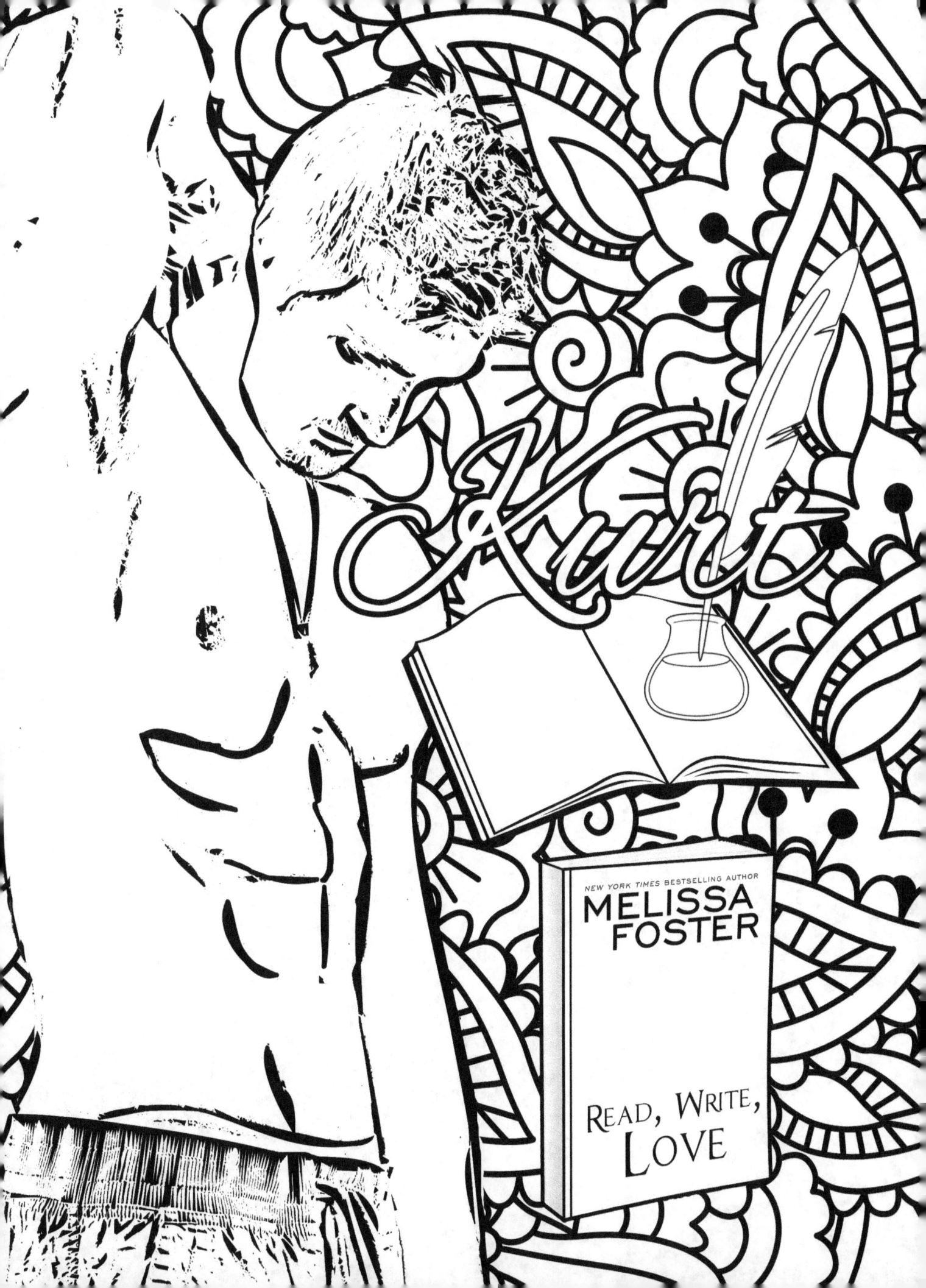

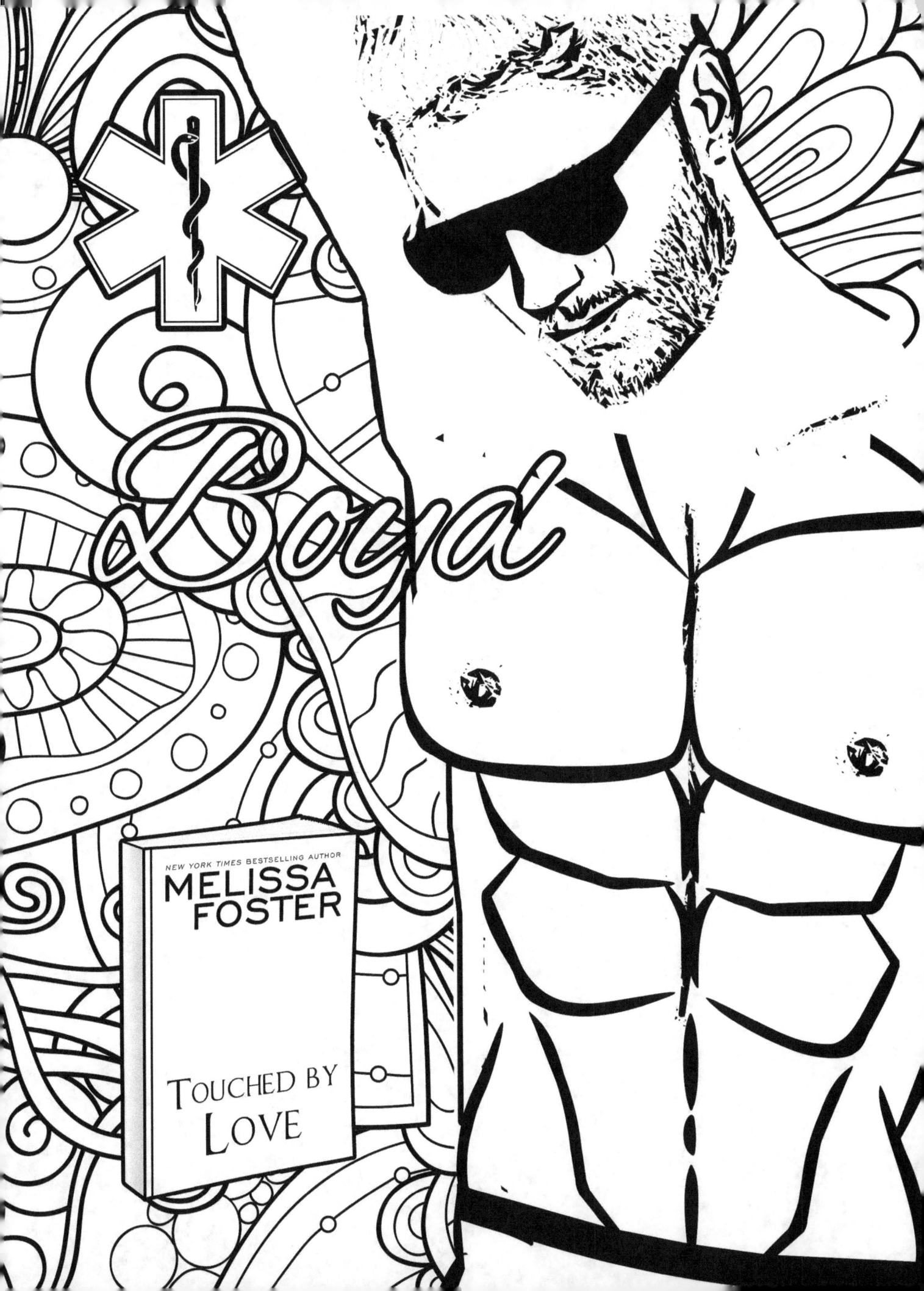

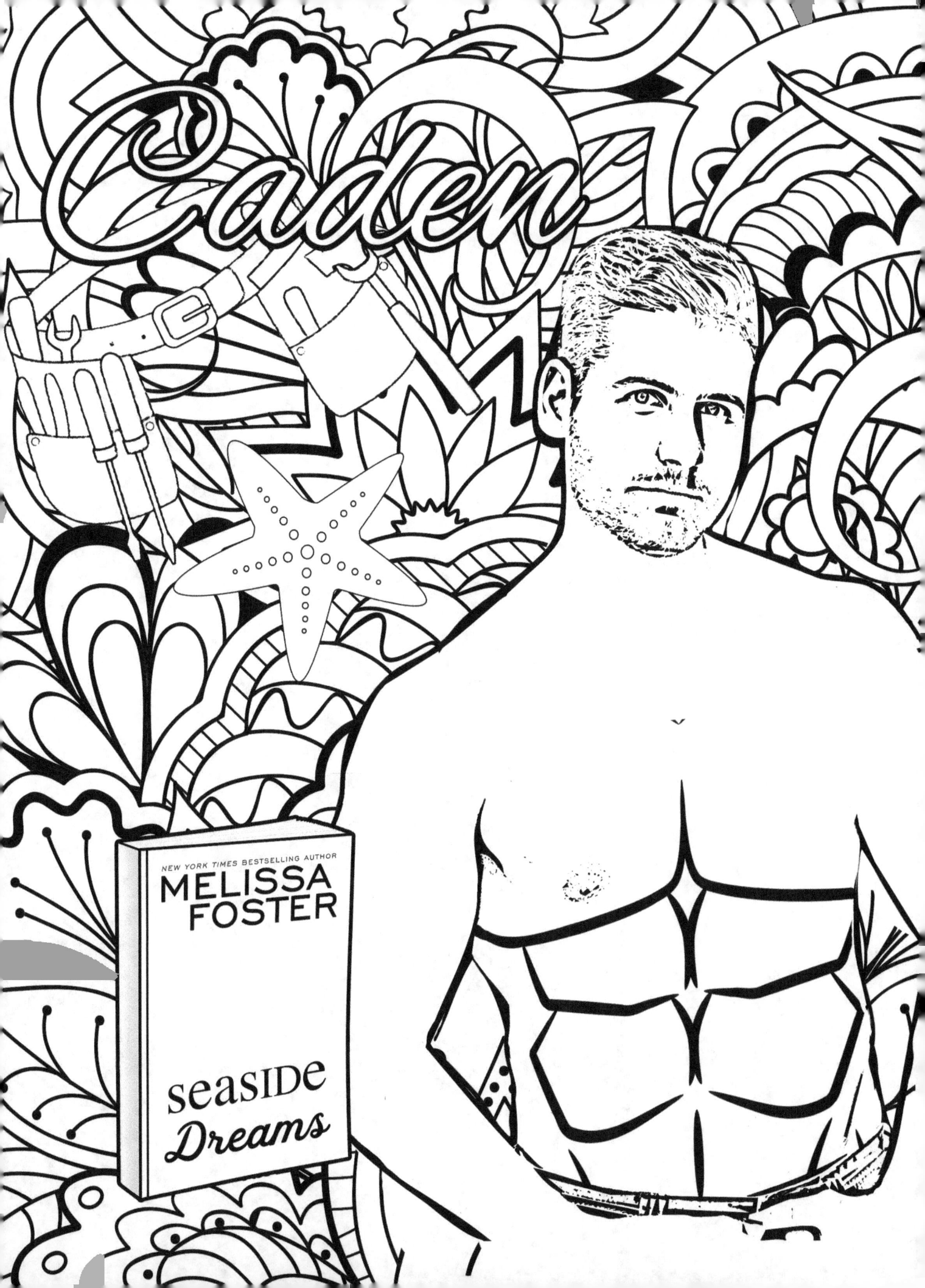

Caden

NEW YORK TIMES BESTSELLING AUTHOR
MELISSA
FOSTER

seaside
Dreams

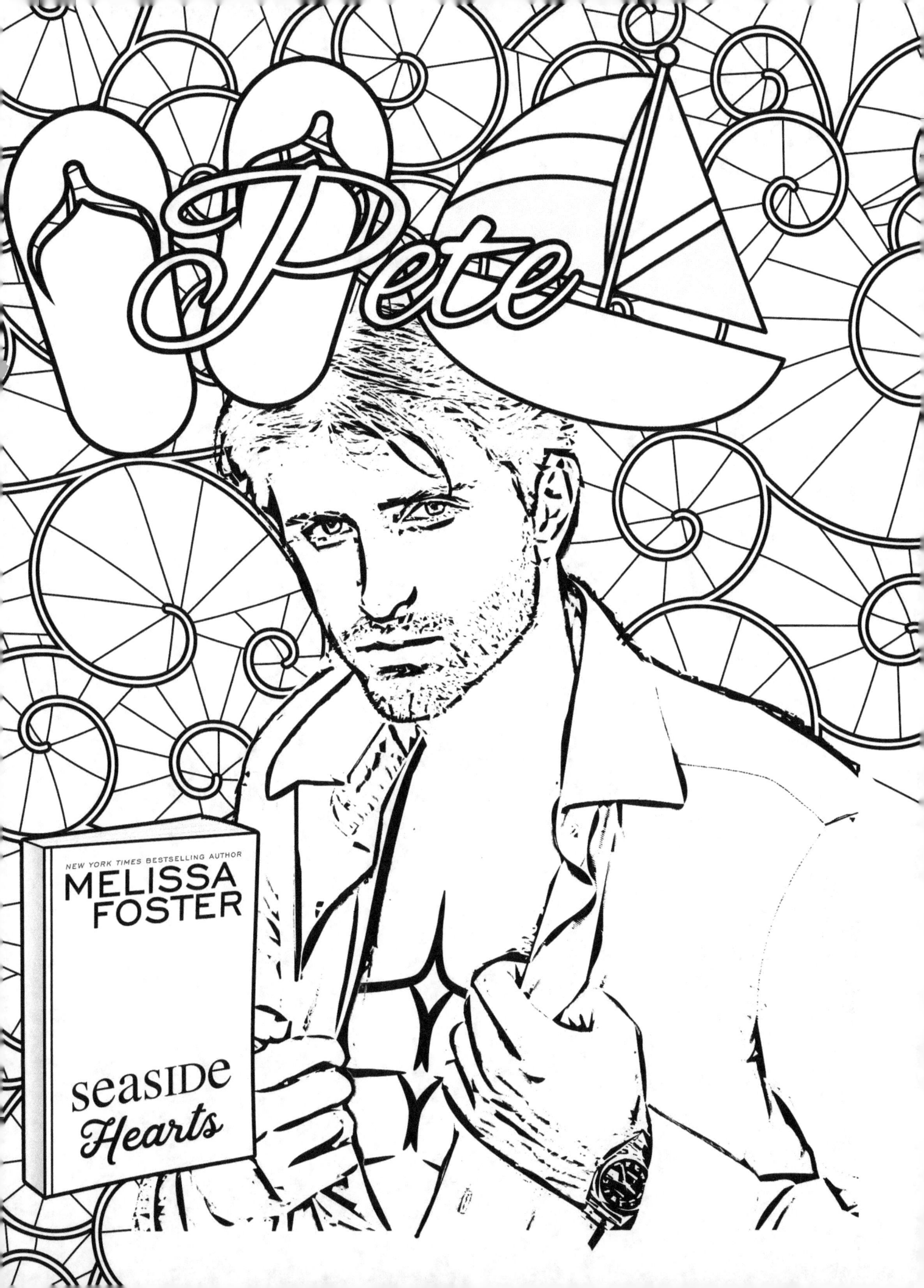

Pete

NEW YORK TIMES BESTSELLING AUTHOR
MELISSA FOSTER

seaside
Hearts

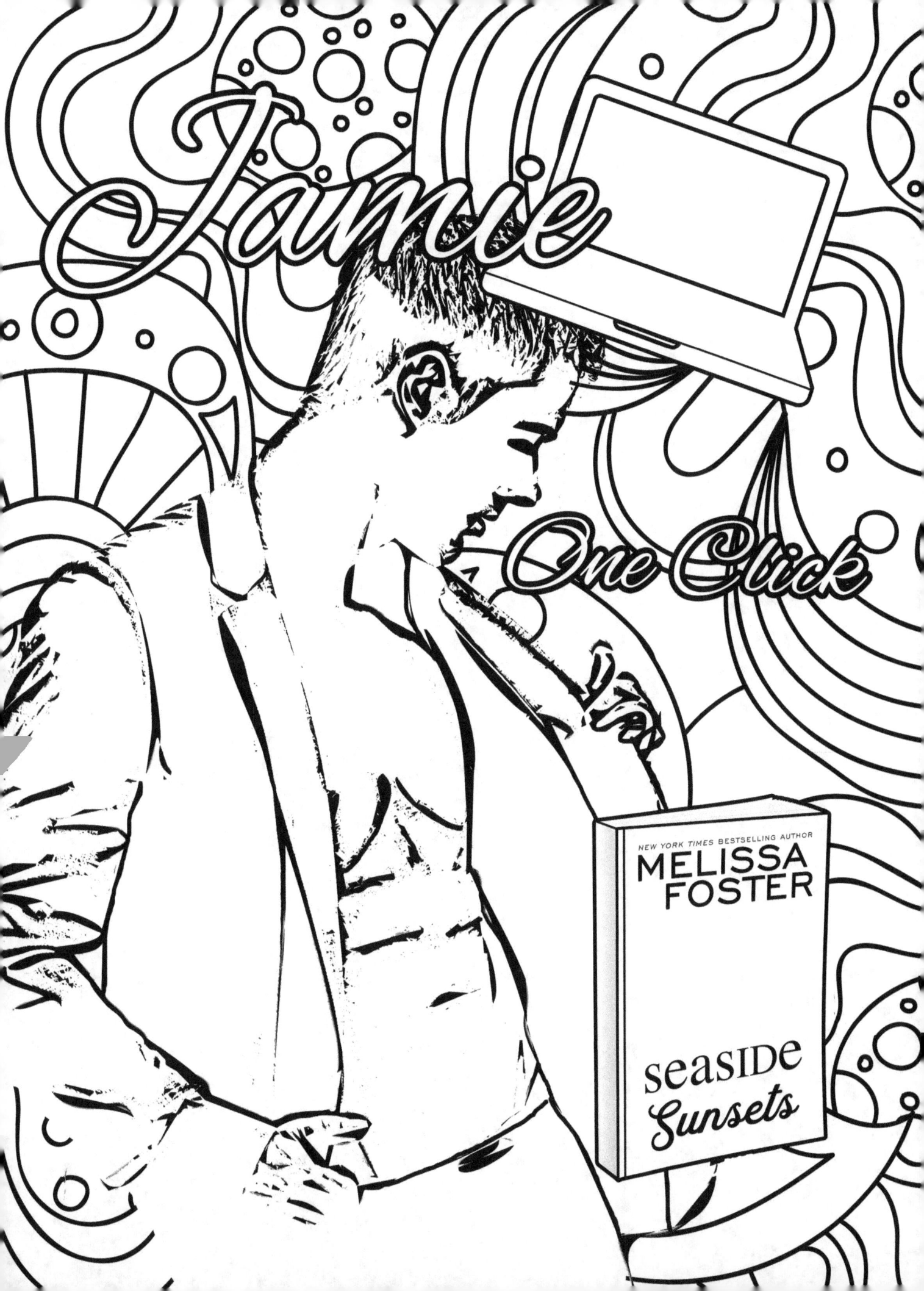

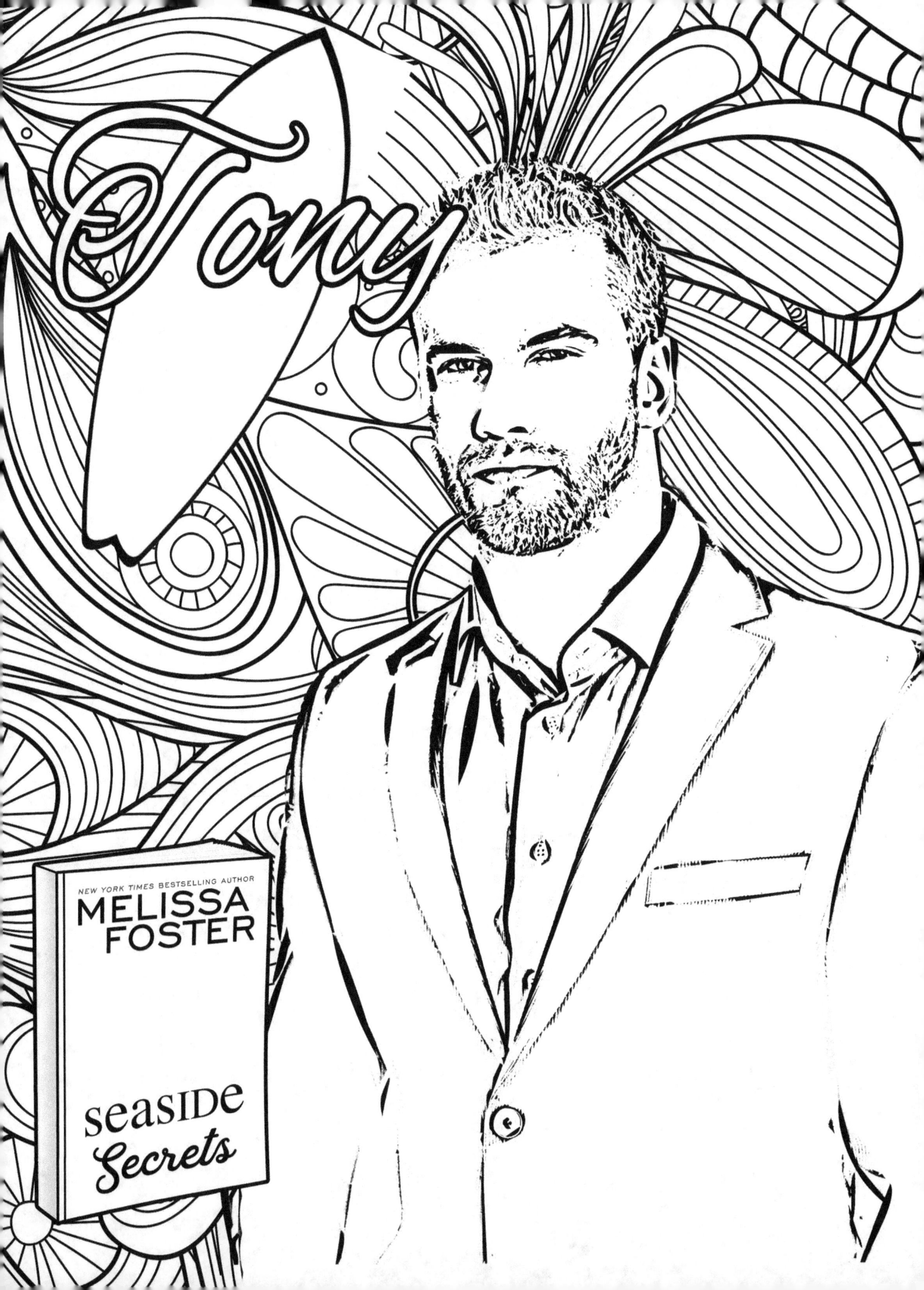

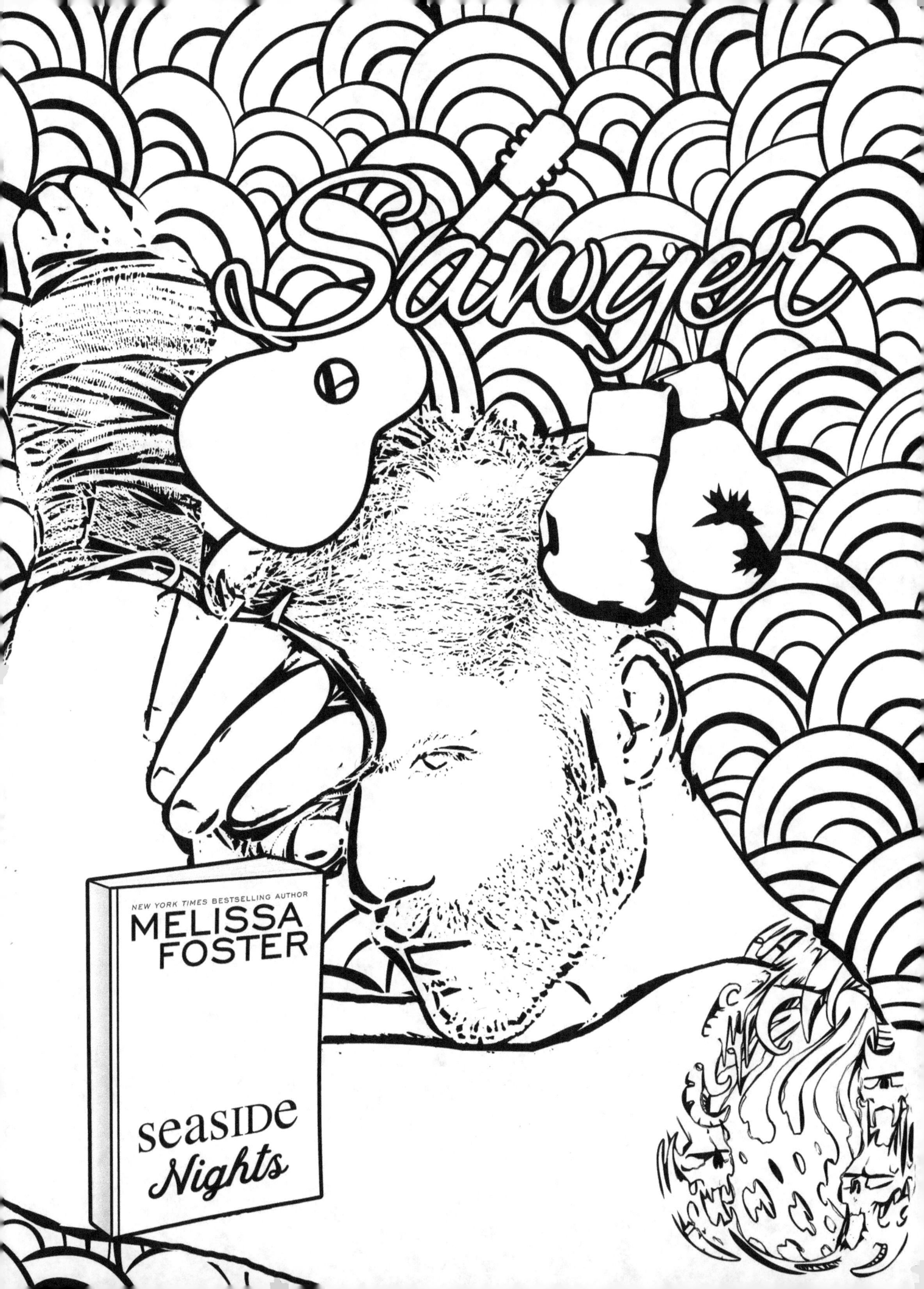

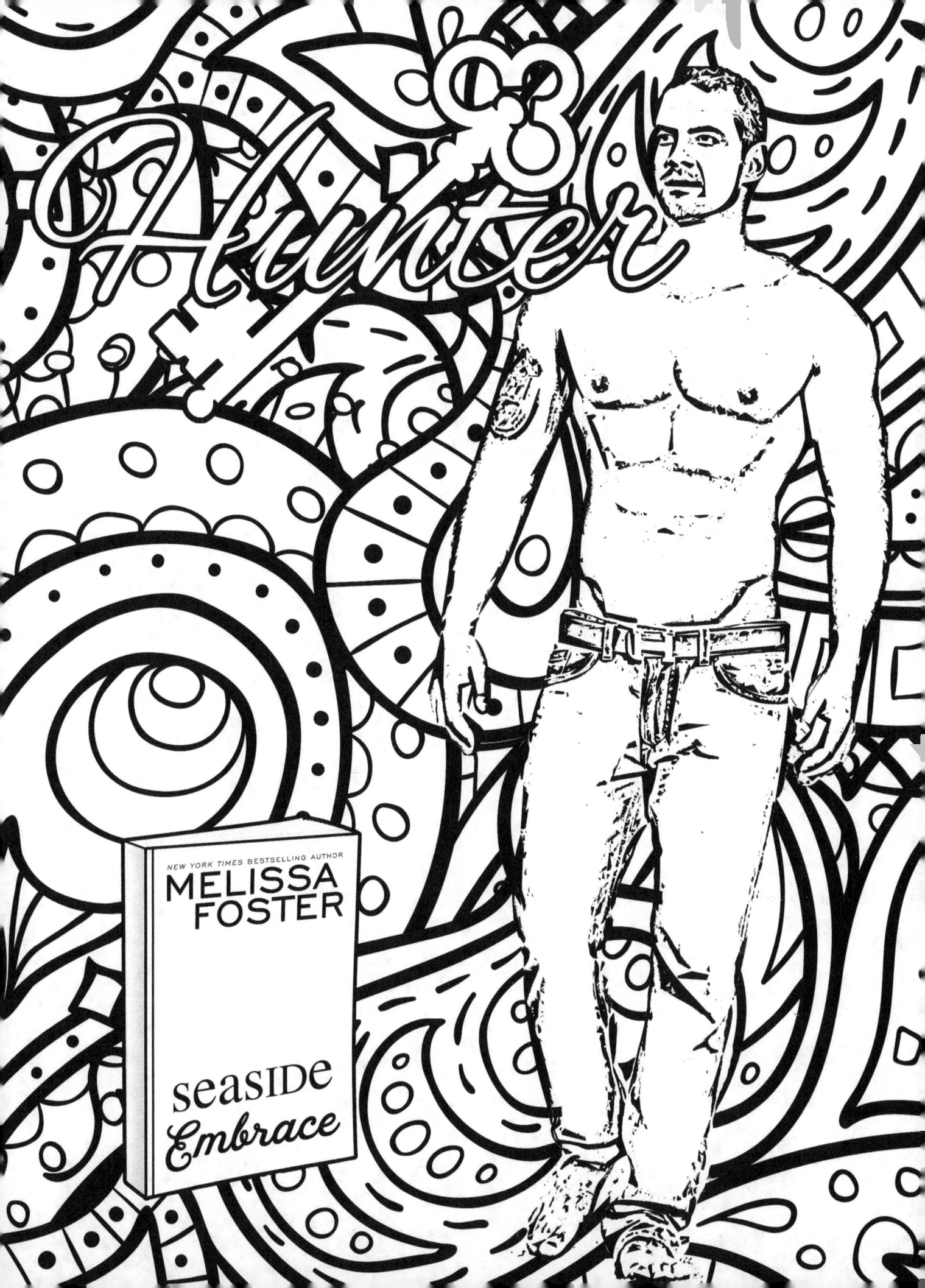

Hunter

NEW YORK TIMES BESTSELLING AUTHOR
MELISSA FOSTER

seaside
Embrace

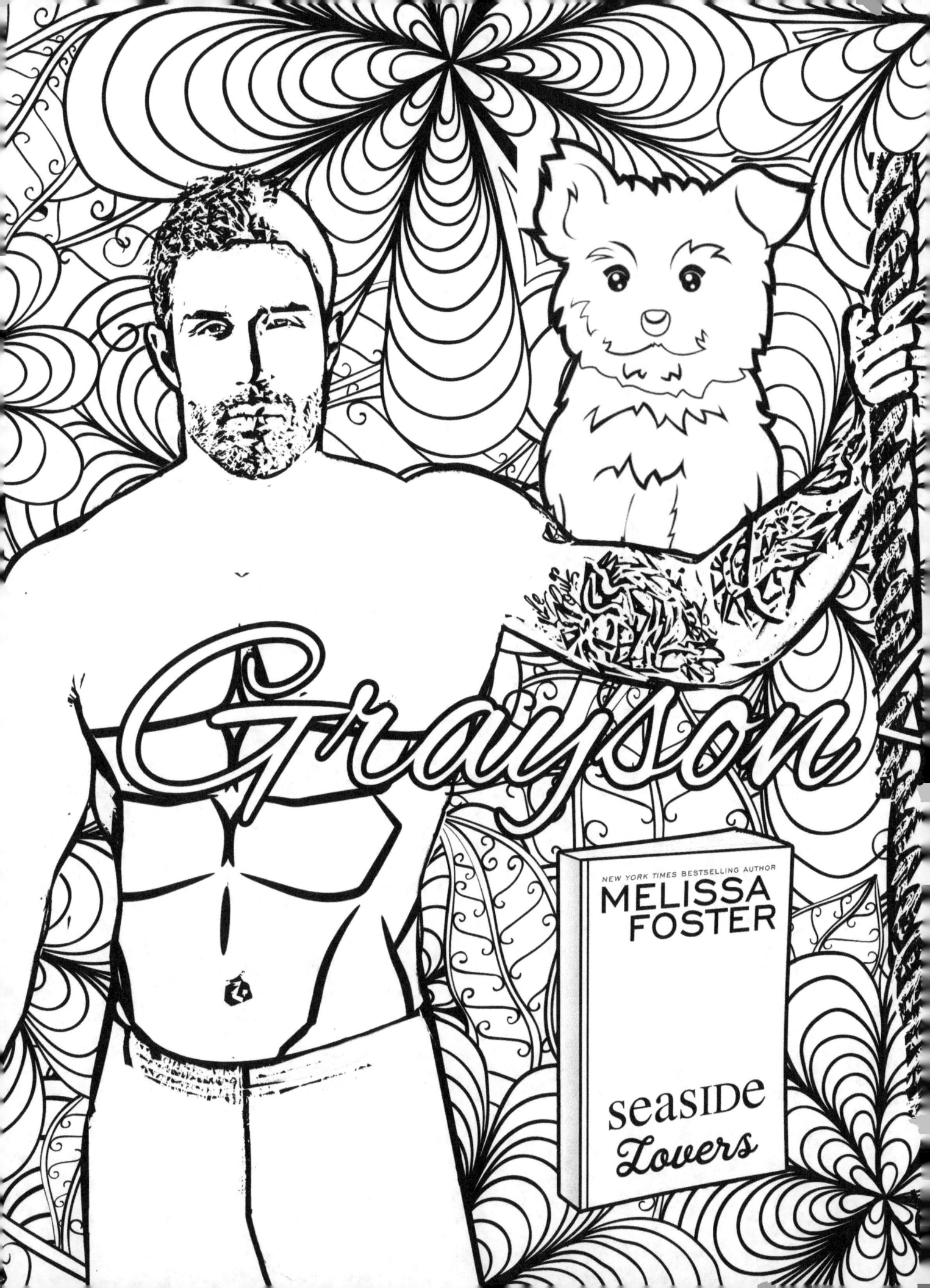

Grayson

NEW YORK TIMES BESTSELLING AUTHOR
MELISSA FOSTER

seaside
Lovers

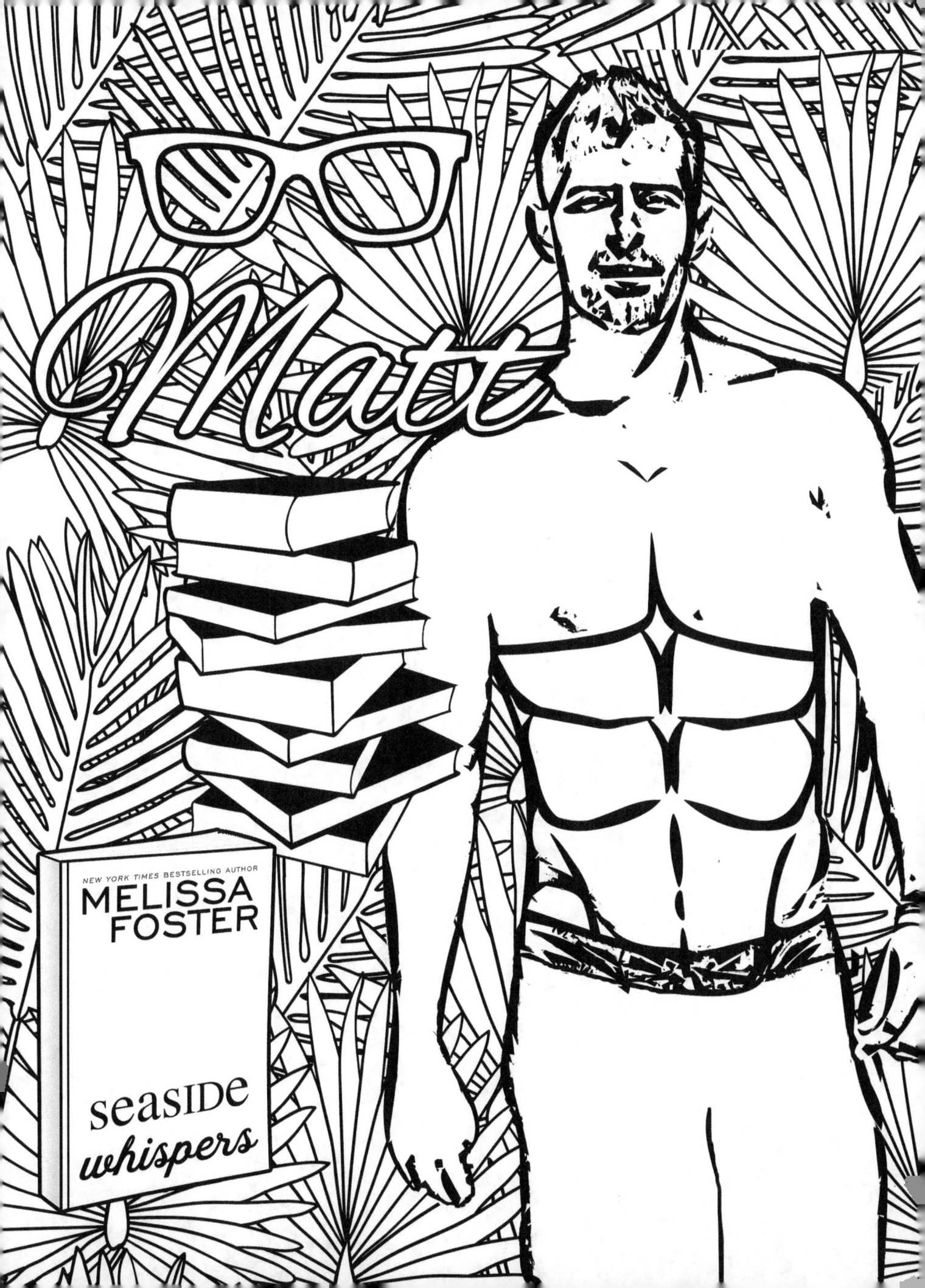

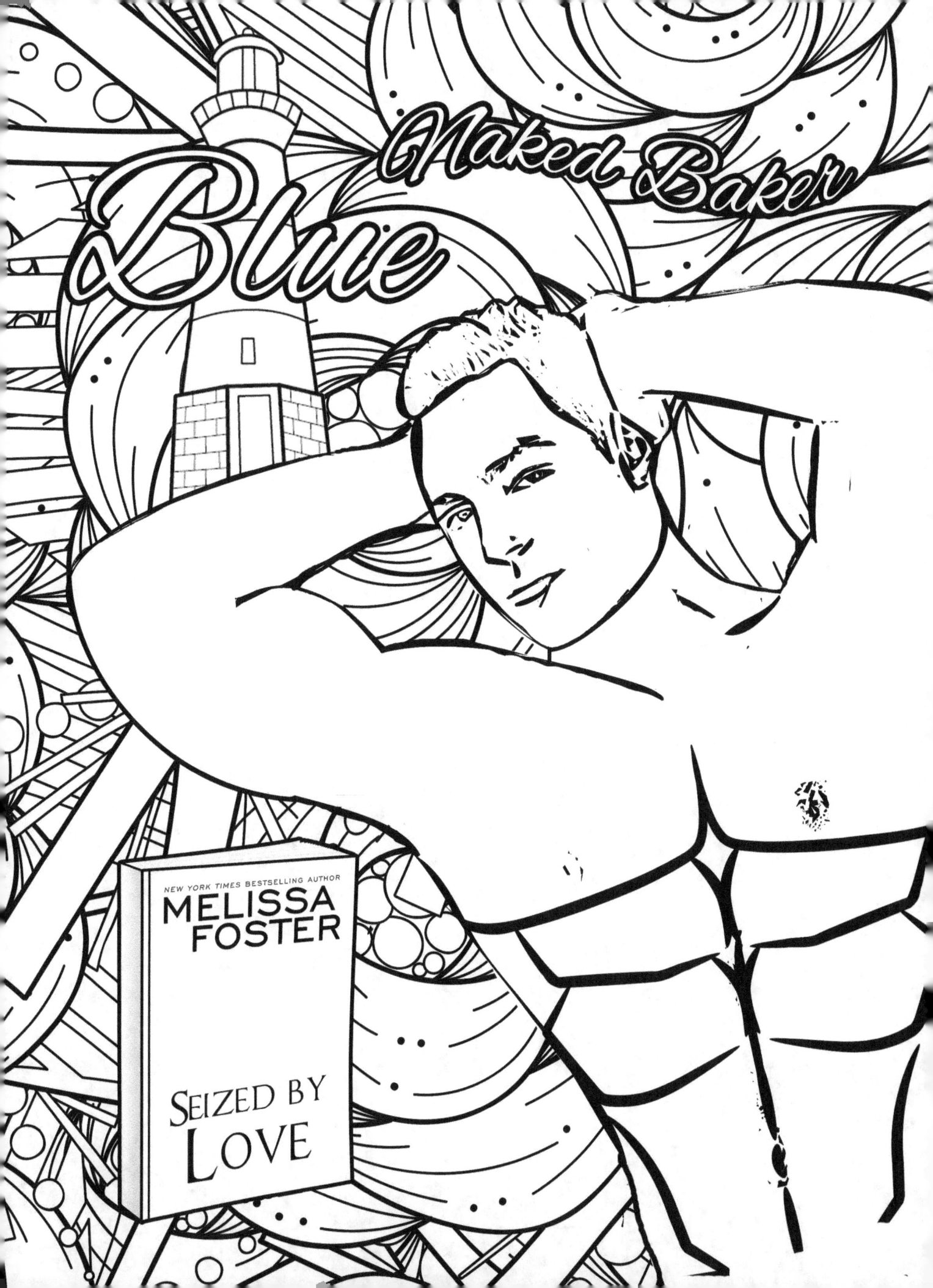

Naked Baker

Blue

NEW YORK TIMES BESTSELLING AUTHOR
MELISSA FOSTER

SEIZED BY
LOVE

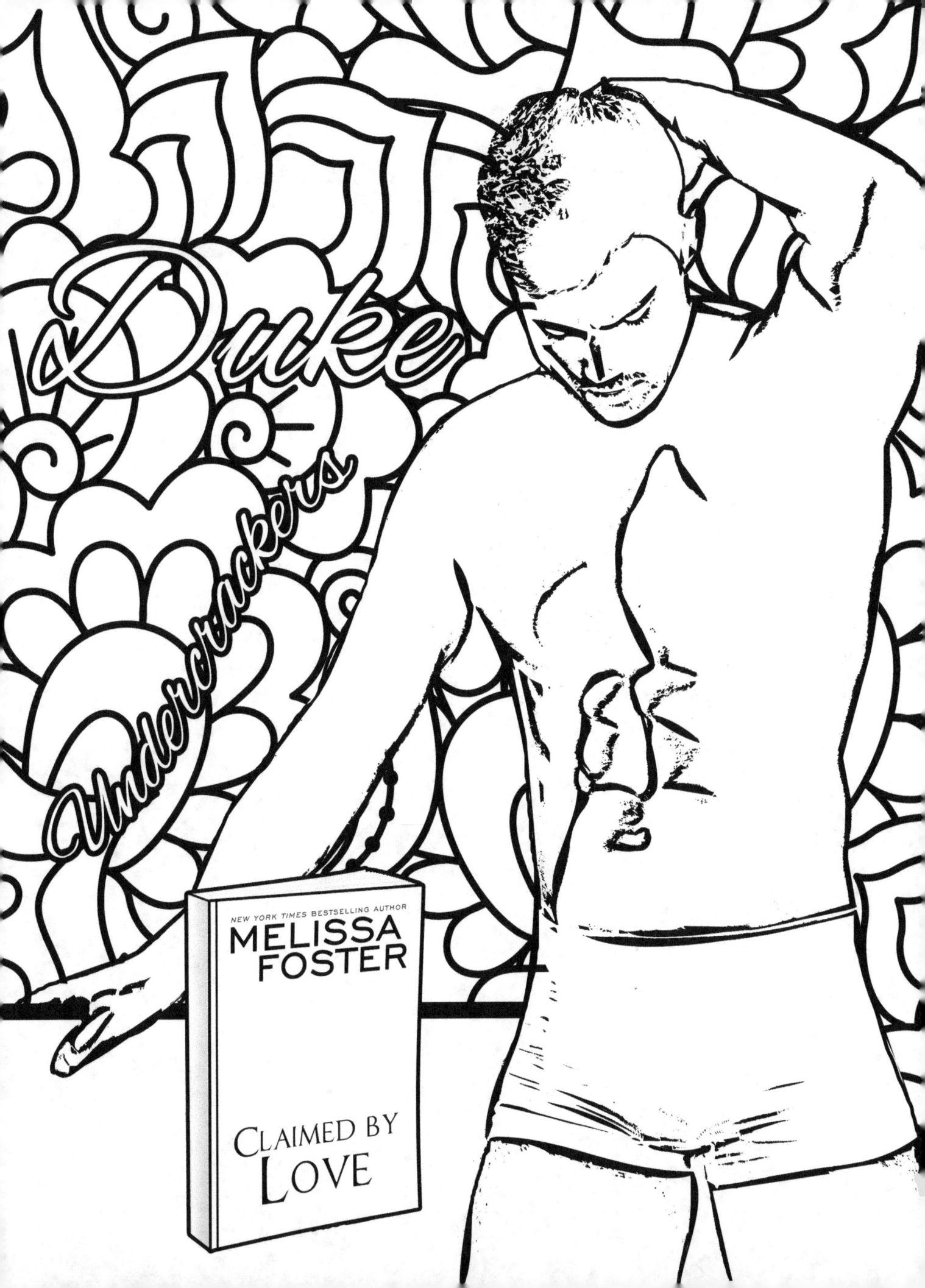

Duke

Undercrackers

NEW YORK TIMES BESTSELLING AUTHOR
MELISSA
FOSTER

CLAIMED BY
LOVE

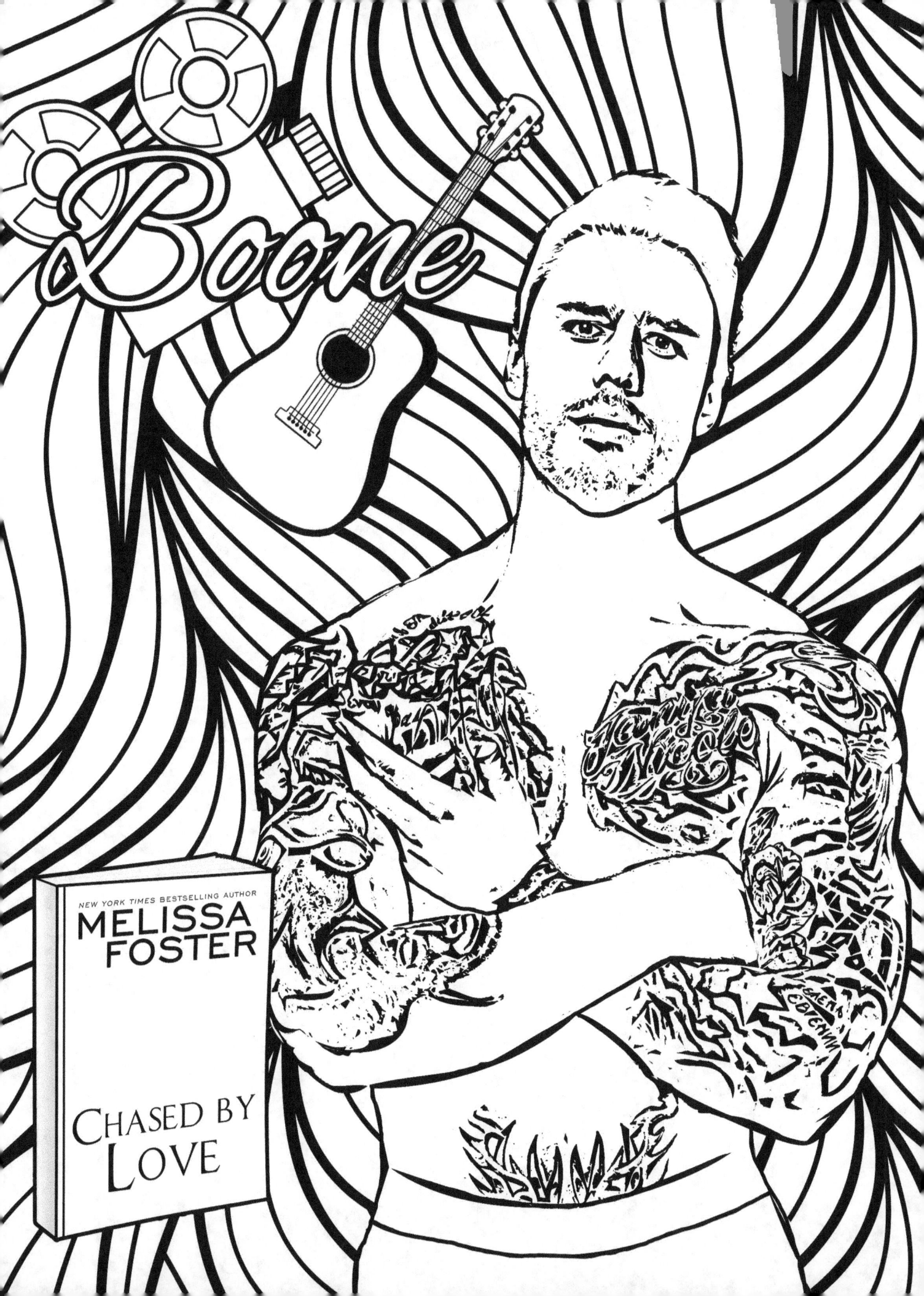

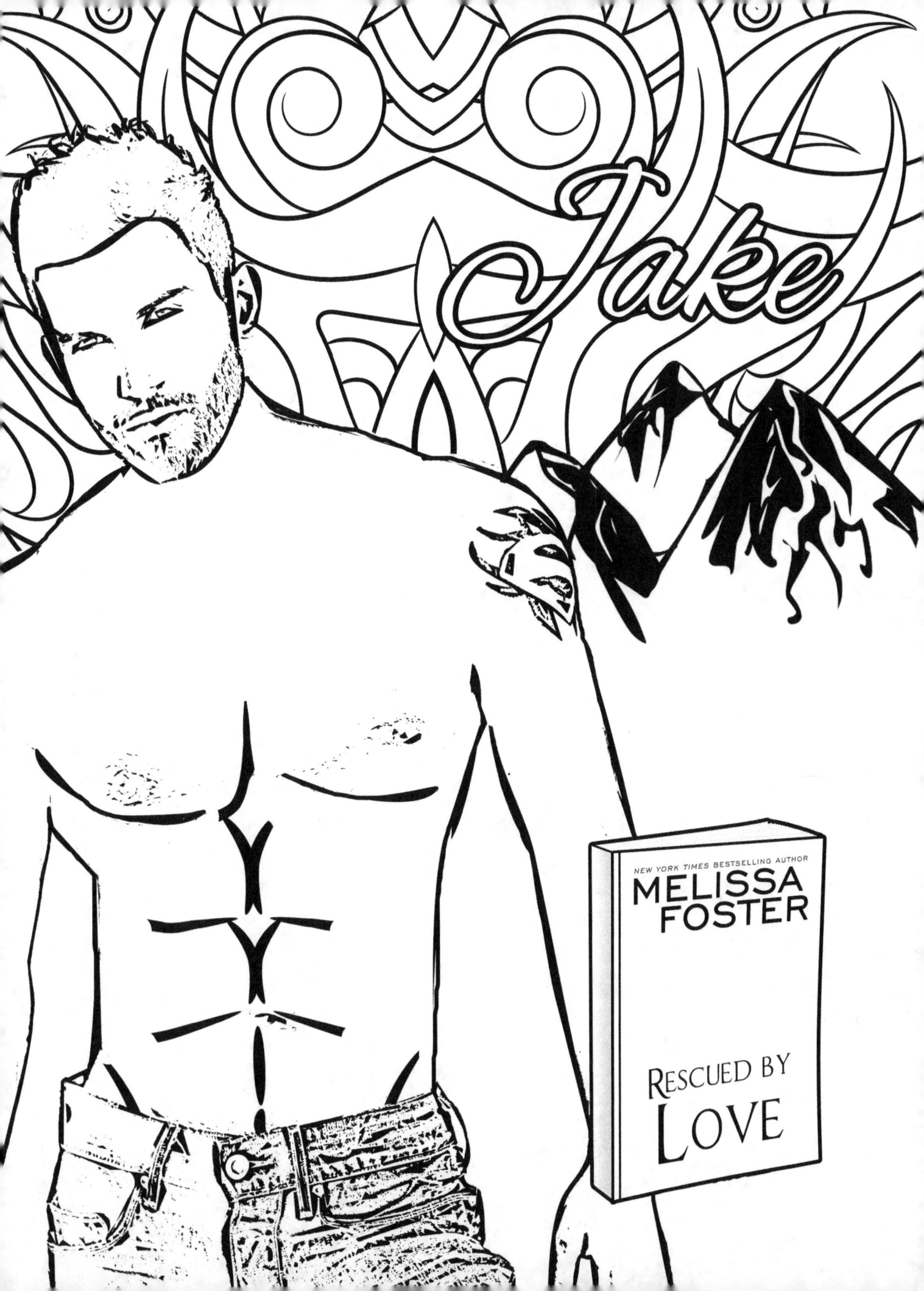

Jake

NEW YORK TIMES BESTSELLING AUTHOR
MELISSA FOSTER

RESCUED BY
LOVE

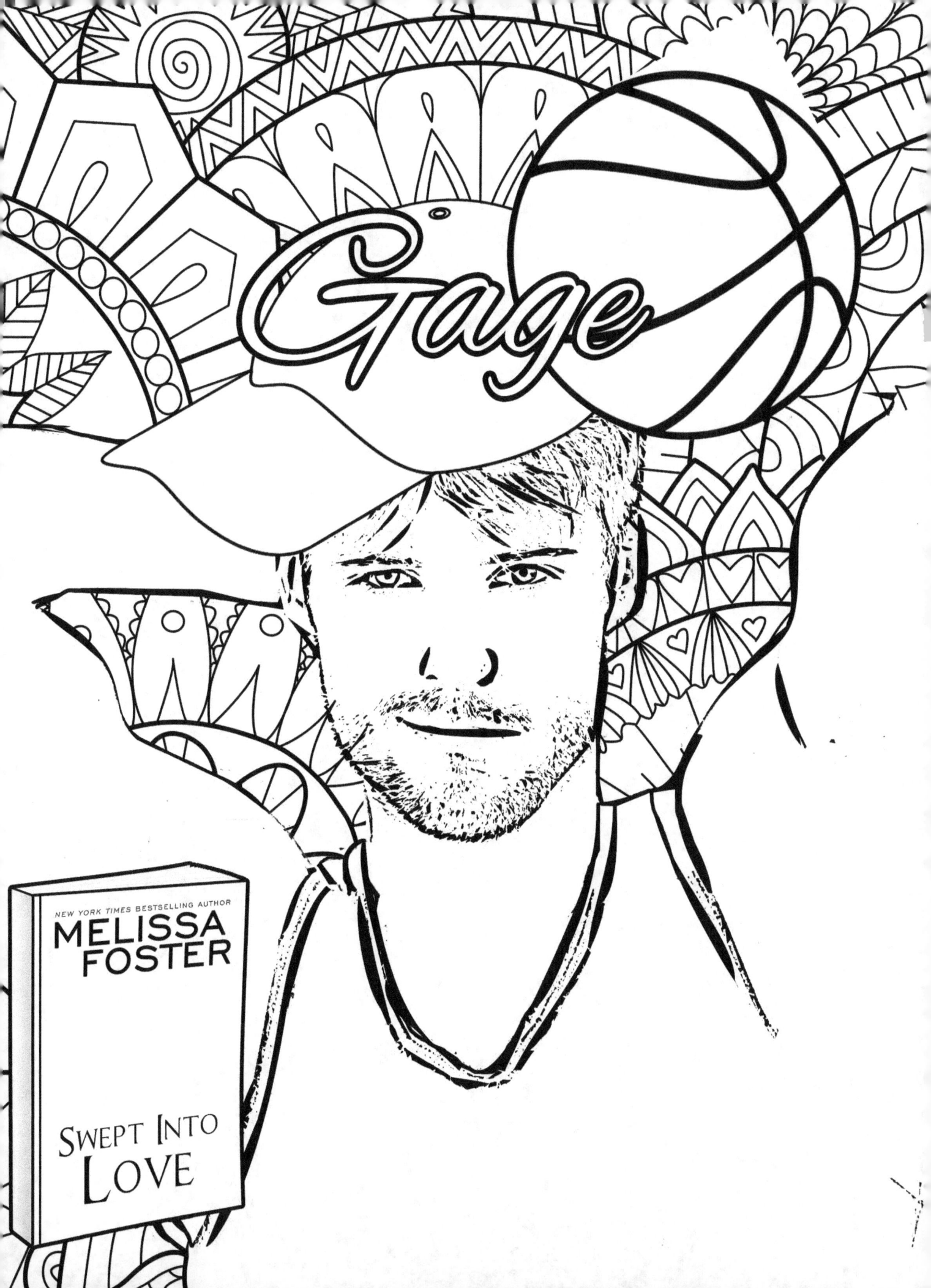

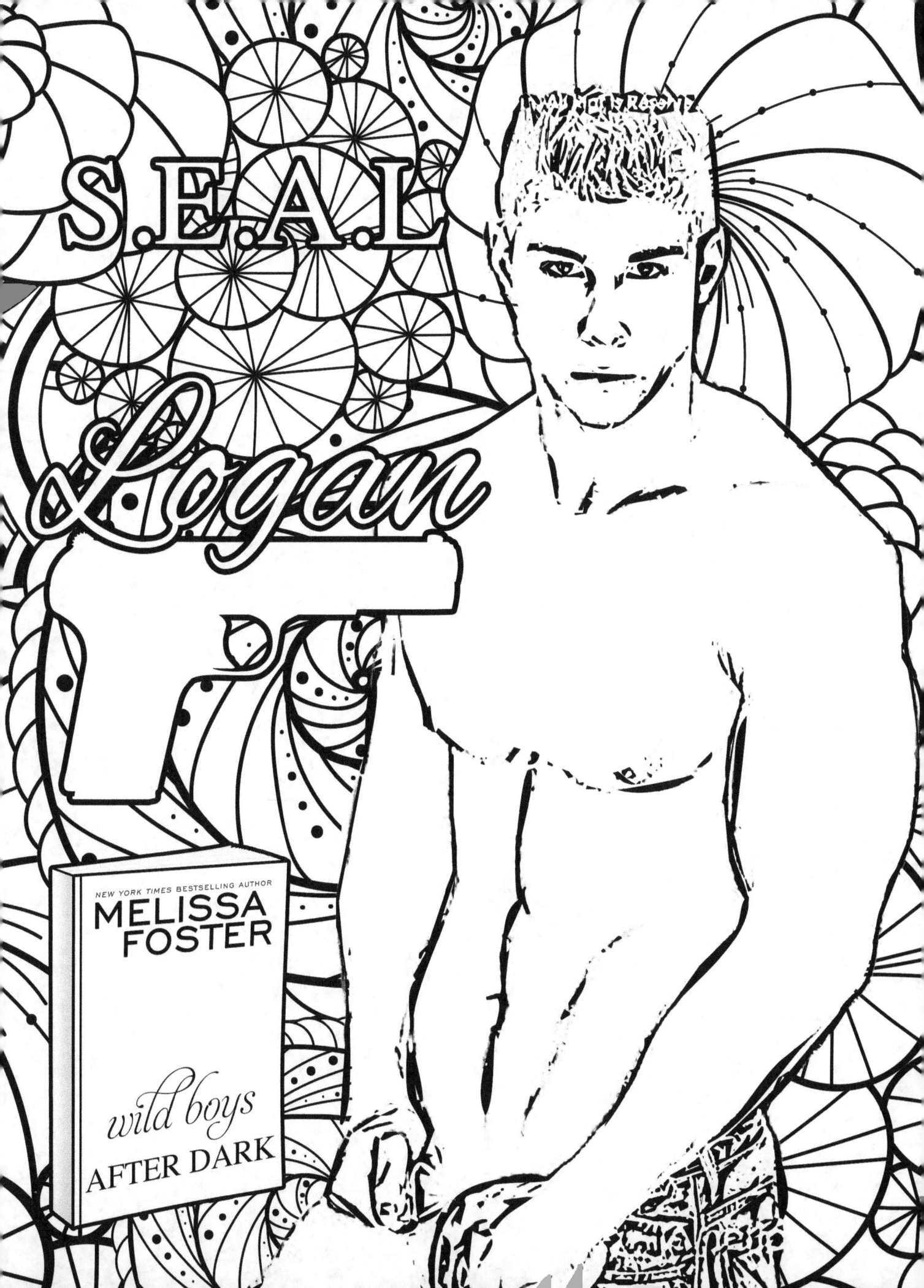

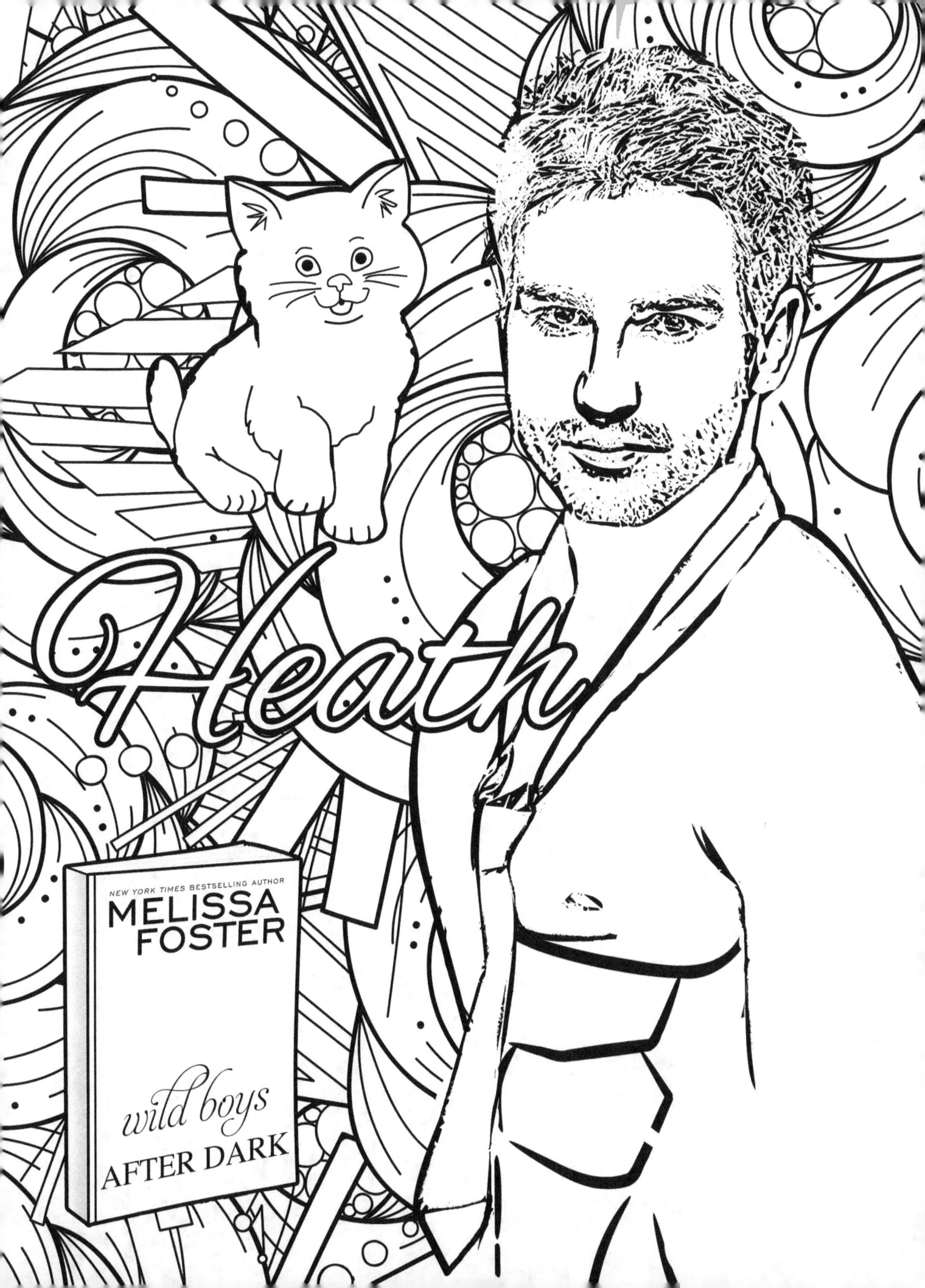

Heath

NEW YORK TIMES BESTSELLING AUTHOR
MELISSA
FOSTER

wild boys
AFTER DARK

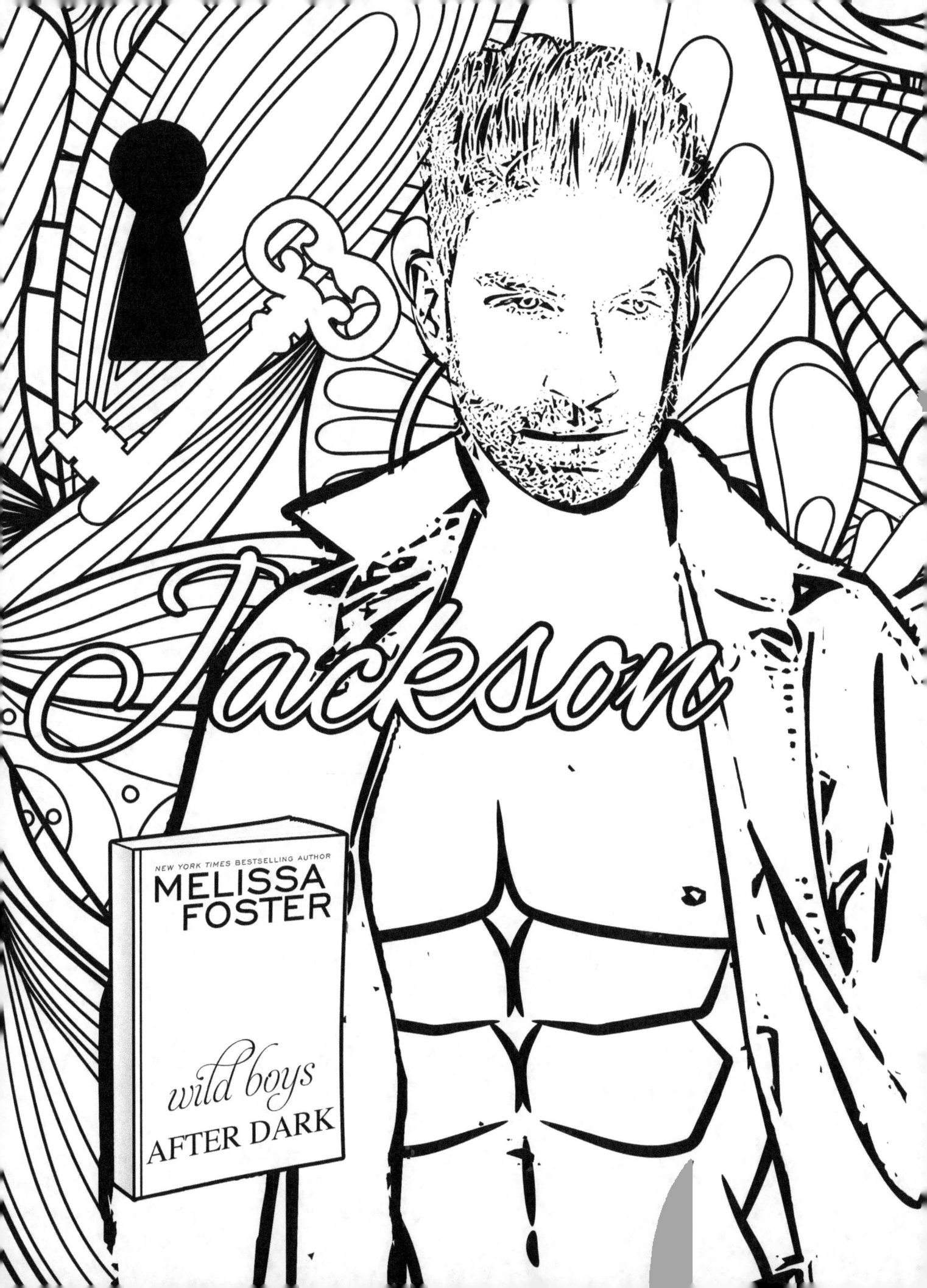

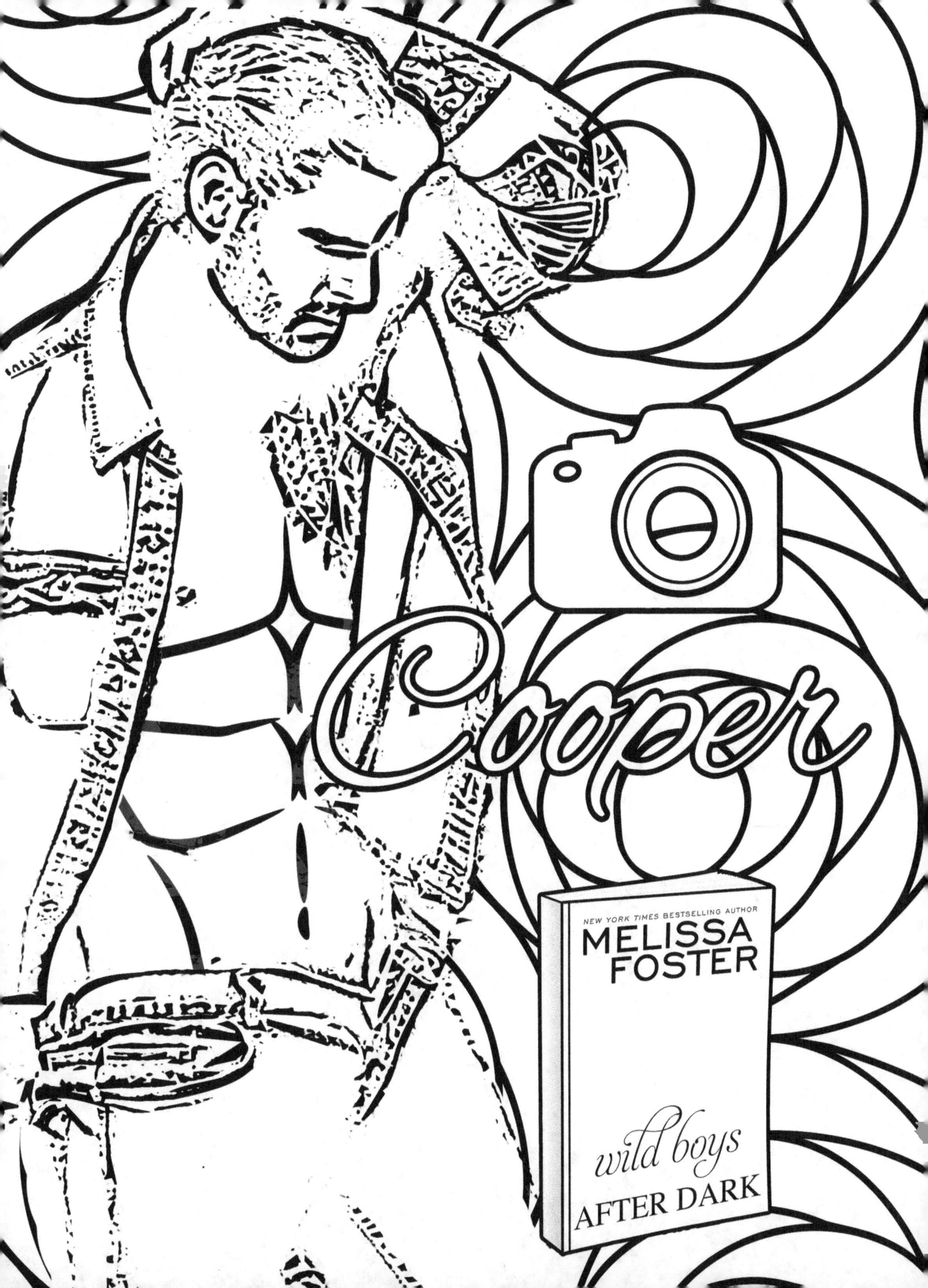

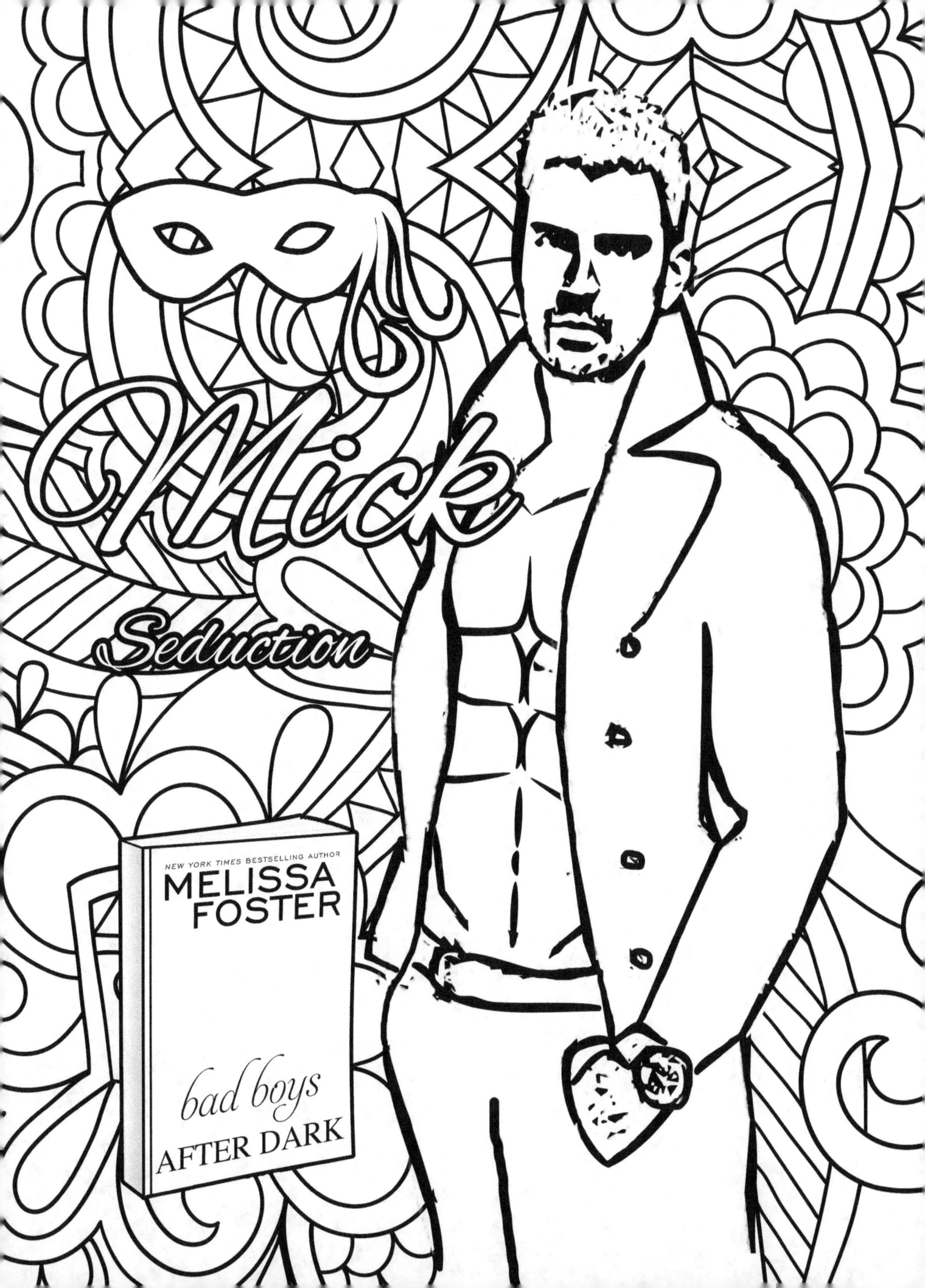

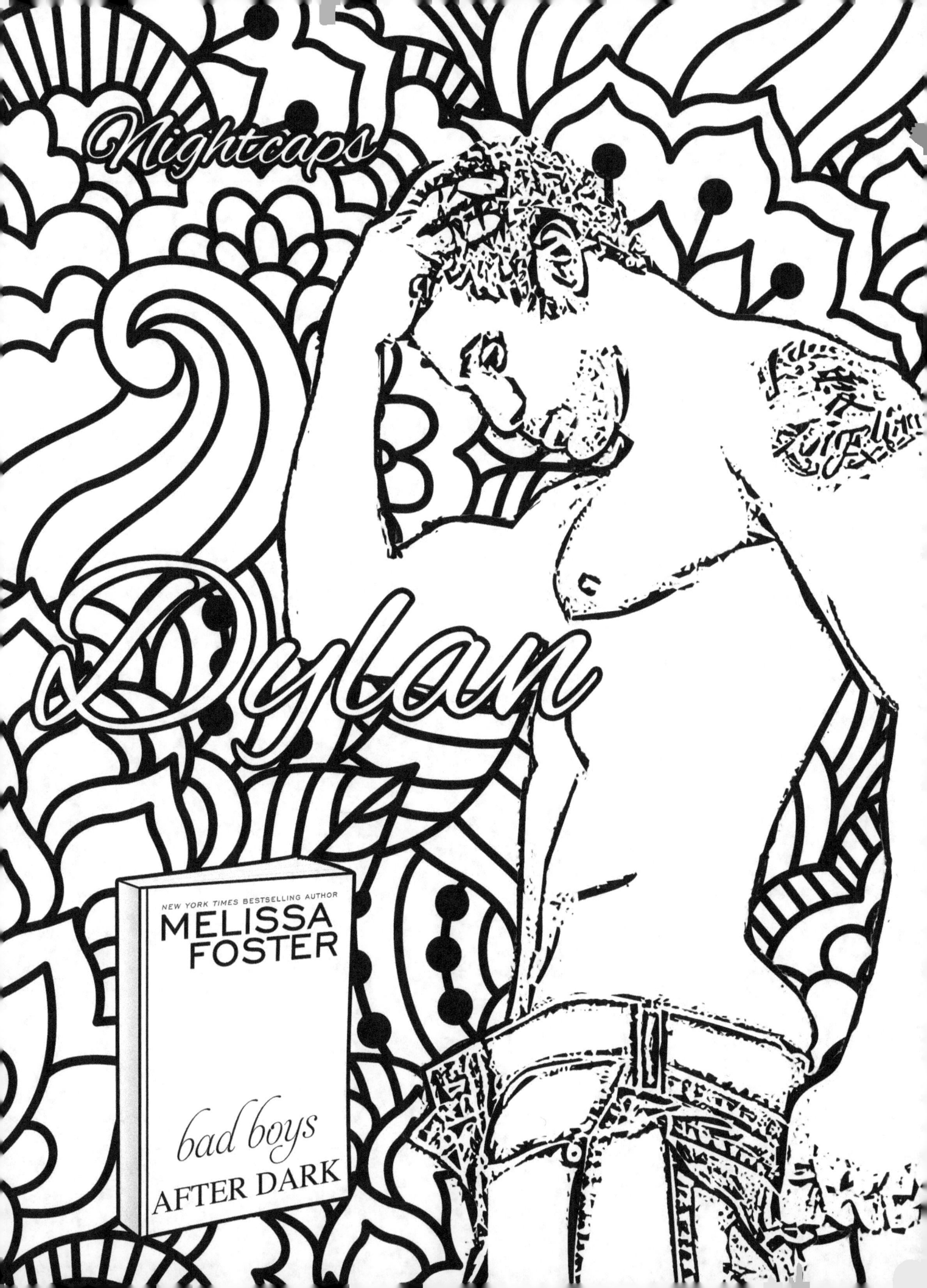

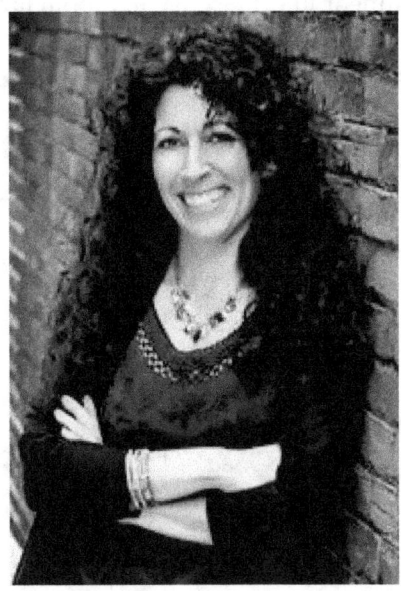

Having sold more than a million books, Melissa Foster is a *New York Times* and *USA Today* bestselling and award-winning author. Her books have been recommended by *USA Today's* book blog, *Hagerstown* magazine, *The Patriot*, and several other print venues. She is the founder of the World Literary Café, and when she's not writing, Melissa helps authors navigate the publishing industry through her author training programs on Fostering Success. Melissa has painted and donated several murals to the Hospital for Sick Children in Washington, DC.

Visit Melissa on her website or chat with her on social media. Melissa enjoys discussing her books with book clubs and reader groups and welcomes an invitation to your event.

Melissa's books are available through most online retailers in paperback and digital formats.

www.MelissaFoster.com
www.MelissaFoster.com/Newsletter
www.MelissaFoster.com/Reader-Goodies

Have you read Melissa's Love in Bloom big-family romance collection?
Each book may be enjoyed as a standalone novel, or read as part of the larger series. Characters from each family appear in other Love in Bloom family series.

For more details on the Love in Bloom series, visit www.MelissaFoster.com

SNOW SISTERS
Sisters in Love
Sisters in Bloom
Sisters in White

THE BRADENS
Lovers at Heart
Destined for Love
Friendship on Fire
Sea of Love
Bursting with Love
Hearts at Play
Taken by Love
Fated for Love
Romancing My Love
Flirting with Love
Dreaming of Love
Crashing into Love
Healed by Love
Surrender My Love
River of Love
Crushing on Love
Whisper of Love
Thrill of Love

BRADEN NOVELLAS
Promise My Love
Our New Love
Daring Her Love

THE REMINGTONS
Game of Love
Stroke of Love
Flames of Love
Slope of Love
Read, Write, Love
Touched by Love

SEASIDE SUMMERS
Seaside Dreams
Seaside Hearts
Seaside Sunsets
Seaside Secrets
Seaside Nights
Seaside Embrace
Seaside Lovers
Seaside Whispers

THE RYDERS
Seized by Love
Claimed by Love
Chased by Love
Rescued by Love
Swept Into Love

SEXY STAND-ALONE ROMANCE
Tru Blue
Wild Whiskey Nights

BILLIONAIRES AFTER DARK
Wild Boys After Dark
Logan
Heath
Jackson
Cooper
Bad Boys After Dark
Mick
Dylan
Carson
Brett

HARBORSIDE NIGHTS SERIES
Includes characters from
Love in Bloom series

Catching Cassidy
Discovering Delilah
Tempting Tristan

Stand-Alone Novels by Melissa

Chasing Amanda (mystery/suspense)
Come Back to Me (mystery/suspense)
Have No Shame (historical fiction/romance)
Love, Lies & Mystery (3-book bundle)
Megan's Way (literary fiction)
Traces of Kara (psychological thriller)
Where Petals Fall (suspense)